"A riot...I nearly split my sides laughing...!"

—**Don Lowe,** (late of) Citrad Ltd[1].

*"Times past are often times present and this small book may still be used to guide the truly adventurous soul who wants to risk life and limb travelling on Jamaica's MAXI minibus "**transpotes**"*

—**Ronnie DQ**[2], Retired U.H. of the West Indies[3] 'Knife Man'

"For anybody who has ever travelled on a bus, this book is a must!"

—**Mike Campbell**, Island Car Rentals[4]

"...vivid and colourful...humorous, surprising, sometimes sad but always intriguing. Makes me look forward to your next book"

—**Angela van der Waals**, Royal Netherlands Embassy[5]

"An uproarious look at growing up on Jamaican public transport"

—**Robert Cleaves**[6], *Vermont winter regular to Jamaica*

Academia! Included in the Jamaican authors series of MoBay Community College[7] & the doctoral thesis references of **Dr. S. Tame Durrleman**[8], *Maitre-asst., U. of Geneva*

---

1. http://www.citrad.com/about.php

2. **http://www.jamaicasportsfishing.com/**

3. http://www.mona.uwi.edu/fms/wimj

4. http://www.islandcarrentals.com/

5. http://www.minbuza.nl/en

6. http://www.onlinecounsellingjamaica.com/forget-death-taxes-make-it-life-tax-write-offs-in-jamaica

7. *http://mbcc.edu.jm/mbcc1/*

8. http://www.unige.ch/lettres/linguistique/enseignantschercheurs/equipeSyntaxe/durrleman.html

Other Books by Susan:
The Brown Phoenix
An Erotic Dialogue from the Indies
Coming Soon
Yu Get Jook!
Diaries of a Jamaican Intern

SHUB DOWN
& SMALL-UP YUSELF!

Diaries of Jamaica by Bus

Written & Illustrated by Susan Lowe
Original Cover Art by Peter Lowe
(Note delicately Gilberted watermark circa 1988)

Polar Bear Press
Jamaica W.I.

---

9. http://www.onlinecounsellingjamaica.com/

10. http://www.facebook.com/pages/Online-Counselling-Jamaica/127528223969280

11. https://twitter.com/#!/OnlineJam

12. http://www.gopublished.com

ACKNOWLEDGEMENTS

(You can skip this page, but there are quite a few people to thank)
Dad for making us take the bus
Mum for typing the first draft
Grandpa who thought we shouldn't take the bus
Aunt Sheila the catalyst
Polar Bear Press for making this possible
Charmaine for friendship & typesetting that went way beyond that job
I did my best to edit this book, so don't blame any of the following kind
people who shared time and suggestions – my mother, Mrs. Hearne, Prof.
Morris, Mr. Rhone, Mrs. Mills, Ronnie, Mike, Angela and Terry
Peter for art editing
Brian Rosen for emergency aid
Burger for a willing spirit...
(Late) Uncle Don for thinking even the first draft was a riot.

FOREWORD

How did we get like this? Just as we're going back to a centralised public transport system precisely because all hell broke loose in Jamaican public transport – wouldn't you like to know? What happened after government couldn't manage to run centralised public transport any more? What proof have we that it can be done now? Read and judge for yourselves.

Here are the first volcanic years of privatised, corporate area, bus transport – the 1970s. During these years the bus system followed the infinite and natural business of the true universal pattern – entropy – order proceeding to chaos. (If you don't sweep cobwebs from your house every week isn't it natural that you'll be overwhelmed by *cobweb an forty-leg*?). Since the universal order is really entropic – with, here and there, the odd enthalpic hiccup of chaos to order – then Jamaica is a very natural place. We're mostly mayhem, and no one, least of all us, should be surprised at us.

After all, as I was profoundly reminded by a *penetrating* dread who mines rain-wash sand and lives in a gully beside one of my past homes; in this country we "Keep that natural regard...".

"Bayswater Omnibus", G.W. Joy – Museum of London

...The passengers change in an omnibus as often in the course of one journey as the figures in a kaleidoscope, and, though not so glittering, are far more amusing. We believe there is no instance of a man's having gone to sleep in one of these vehicles... Again: children, though occasionally, are not often to be found in an omnibus; and even if they are, if the vehicle be full as is generally the case, somebody sits on them, and we are unconscious of their presence. Yes, after mature reflection and considerable experience, we are decidedly of the opinion, that of all known vehicles, from the glass-coach in which we are taken to be christened, to that sombre caravan in which we must one day make our last earthly journey, there is nothing like an omnibus.

"Sketches by Boz", Dickens

Come now Mr. Dickens, mek
me tell yu how it really go...

EN ROUTE

1

Route 67

"Yu kyaan come in wid all dem heap o someting yu know!!"

All the regulars, passengers and crew, really got to know each other on Route 67. It was actually a route for helpers and school children. Wolmers, Campion, Providence, Sts. Peter and Paul, Liguanea and St. Margaret's Preps all had featured roles. Everyone knew where everyone else's home was.

As well as the star characters, the group included some of the most thoughtful and polite people you could possibly meet. If it was raining, regular passengers were often picked up between stops and old people were waited on and helped to board and get off the buses. One crew was exceptional in its care. Well behaved students and polite grownups who were usually on time at their morning stops earned a special wait of up to five minutes so that they wouldn't miss their bus. If a little brother or sister didn't show up, the conductress would ask why and, if he or she were sick, say how sorry she was. When the child got better the conductress gave him or her a big welcome smile and a friendly chat.

Like I said, when it first opened, Route 67 was worked by and carried some real characters. We once had a conductress with some serious priorities.

Mostly empty as usual, the bus was rushing along – around Matilda's Corner, up Widcombe Road and then – the favourite Monterey run. All of a sudden, the conductress leapt out of her seat, as if something had bitten her, screaming, "STAP DE BUS! STAP DE BUS!" She clacked a coin wildly on the handlebar and everyone turned round in horror to see what disaster had struck. The woman was on her feet holding on to the vertical hand rail and dancing around like *spirit tek er*.

"ME SAY FE STAP DE BUS!"

Had somebody fallen out?! Been run over?! **What**, my God??!!

The bus screeched to a stop outside Mr. Carlton's house and gassed us with stinking rubber fumes. The door was bashed open and the driver jerked round in horror.

There was a big mango tree in the front garden and a helper was standing in the front door of the house. The conductress raced to the bus door bawling out at the top of her lungs, "Y' AVE ANY MANGO FE SALE?!" There was dead silence.

"HU-RASS!" shouted the shocked driver and every other mouth let fly every kind of disbelief - and there's not much that surprises Jamaicans.

"Is mad yu mad, nuh, oman?!", inquired the driver of the conductress over his shoulder. "A dead yu gwine dead we fe mango? **Mchchchch!"** He rammed in the gear and was looking studiously into his side mirror as he drove off.

"Nuh talk to me Man, shut yu mout and jive de bus!" was the reply. Other passengers who also tried, loudly, to point out the folly of her actions were met with disdain and a resounding kissing of teeth.

One afternoon, at least four characters put on a serious Route 67 show. 'Speedy' was at the wheel. Route 67 passengers gave him this name because he seemed hell bent on achieving his missed calling – that of a Formula I race driver. Backing him up was his hefty co-worker, a big old conductress who sat in her back seat, no smile, looking like a buddha who only came to life at odd times. Their passengers included the usual motley bunch of day workers, jobbers and students who had just burst the Friday afternoon flood-gates.

Buddha handled it all with her usual stone face, ripping out the tickets from the dispenser and returning the change like an assembly line robot.

Then came Douglas...and a bicycle. The khaki Zulu-in-chief. Yes Lord, she knew this one! He had no manners and noisily, proudly and offensively shared his flatulence with the rest of the bus load and sat in the back left corner by an open window. This was the best look-out point a trouble-maker could pick to cause the most problems and get support from or provoke his audience whether inside or outside the bus. This spot was also near his favourite victim – the conductress. His voice was amazingly loud and booming for someone so young.

In the middle of her programme, ticket and 5-cent piece in hand, Buddha stopped. "Yu not comin on."

She came to life – the way she showed signs of it. Her arms hung like boat fenders at her side and her legs were like pylons and almost the same width apart. She had turned full face to the door, blocking the passage of Douglas and his bike. He looked almost surprised. Very few people ever caused him to change the course of his actions. Buddha's head was tilted backwards, her eyebrows made an upside down 'V' and her mouth was an upside down 'U'. Grim. Her arms were folded and jammed under her big bosom and over her large belly. The hyper-extended knees had on the well known reverse arc deadlock.

"Me say yu not comin on wid dat."

Sizing up his situation, Douglas used his best Queen's English and said, "Move aside Lady, I'm not riding up Widcombe today", and, as a ridiculous afterthought, because the tyre was clearly quite okay, "...And furthermore, my dear woman, can't you see the tyre is punctured?"

"Dat tyre nuh look like nuttin nuh do it to me an Me nuh business wha you ave fe say to me...you an it not comin on."

By this time the bus load had begun to giggle and snicker and Speedy was gunning the accelerator. Douglas tried forcing an entry again only to be stopped in his tracks. He raised the universal finger, and, in polite afternoon tea tones, said, "Fuck you Fatty, fuck you. Kyah! Kyah! Kyah! Kyah!...inserting himself into the limelight, again.

The entire bus exploded with laughter as Buddha snorted, "Humph!" and pressed the buzzer. Doors slammed shut, Speedy rammed in the gear and the bus jerked forward. Buddha had already dropped into and overflowed her seat comfortably. She steadied her conductress's caroaches with a meaty hand and grabbed the seat railing in front with the other. Yes, boy! She knew Speedy was at the wheel so she just set her face and prepared for the worst.

He managed to completely rev out first and second gears of the fully loaded Jolly in the couple hundred yards between Matty Corner Police Station and the traffic lights at the intersection up the road. Speedy then heaved the bus through Matilda's Corner and, taking it to third and fourth gear, refused to gear down for the big bend on Barbican road just ahead. Everyone was pitched all over the place grabbing hats, bags and rails for dear life. They were then immediately flung forward as Speedy screeched tyres into the Lane Plaza stop a few hundred yards ahead.

Buddha mumbled, "But is wha do dis man eeh, Sah?"

Older folk and some well brought up youngsters were grumbling – everyone else was having a ball. Speedy, seen in his rear-view mirror, looked well pleased. The doors clapped open with a shattering, tinny noise above the roaring of the high revving engine. An ancient woman began to struggle up the steps with all her bag-an-pan. The pan happened to be an uncapped tin of kerosene oil. Buddha arranged herself for the afternoon's second confrontation, except that, since the woman was old, Buddha didn't completely bar the doorway. She stood with one boat fender hanging by her side, the other akimbo with ticket dispenser sticking out at right angles from it.

"Listen nuh Lady, yu kyaan come in a de bus wid all dem whole eap o someting yu know."

"Lahd! Do mi love, Me's a hole oman, tek time wid me nuh – do!"

"Lady! If Me was fe tek time wid evry smaddy wha…"

"A know mi love, but see wid me nuh – do!"

"Lady, yu nuh see de kersene pan nuh ave nuh top? It wi dash way in a de bus!"

"A know mi love, but see wid me nuh – do," all the while lumbering her caroaches, piece by piece, into the bus.

Neither the huge conductress nor anyone else lifted a finger to help her. It was a sin, but the kerosene was damn' dangerous! The conductress kept up the necessary stream of chiding over everyone's heads and towards the bus front but made no move to stop the old lady. We all understood and the old lady settled herself shakily, pointed bottom first, into the bus seat.

"Oyyy Lahd! Tank yu mi love, God bless yu, God wi bless yu fe de ole lady."

Buddha settled back into her seat, satisfied that she had blustered enough and then, making sure everybody heard, "*Humph!* Me nuh know is why Me ave fe bear all dem worry an crosses y'ear Sah, a-oh. Humph! ...Look ow long Me deh tell de oman say she kyaan come in a de bus wid..."

"Me know, mi love. Gahd wi bless you fe de ole lady."

"Humph! God naah go bless wha Me know say a go appen."

Speedy rammed in second gear and you could tell by the sound of the struggling engine that he couldn't wait to get past the incline of Widcombe Road. The engine revved to an ear splitting scream, but the load wouldn't permit speed. Everybody, already rowdy and in high spirits, screamed as Speedy swung and jerked round the corner at Monterey Drive.

"CRANG!" Kerosene stank up the bus and shouts of, "Is wha de backside...?!! Jeezas Chris!" and "Go deh Speedy, go deh!" echoed in the bus. A folder slapped open on the floor, loose leaves flew out.

With a movement that, in most people, was equal to jumping out of their seats and shouting with I-told-you-so satisfaction, Buddha raised a hand, slapped her knee', threw back her head and said, "Coo deh now! See it deh?! Is wha Me did tell you? Me know, man, Me know! Nuh *mus*??!!"

"Is ahright dahlin, Me wi wipe it up man, nuh fret."

Speedy didn't let up one inch. The thrill of Monterey was in his blood. Third and fourth gear were drawn with dashing double clutch. We barrelled down like a caboose gone mad.

Over the roar, the conductress shouted her command, "Beg yu sidung y'ear Ma, an mek dis ya eediot do wha im a do... But Lahd Jeezas ave Is mercy, wha mek wid dis ya man dis ahftanoon, Sah?!"

"Ahright Ma, Me wi cork it up fe yu, nuh worry," croaked the old woman. She tore up some newspaper covering the bankra she had, screwed it up and stuffed it into the kerosene tin's spout. Yes boy...a wick!

"Lady, it goin dash way again yu know, specially as how dis ya eediot a drive like if im ear news. Beg yu ole on to it fe me, yaah Ma!

The breeze blasted through the bus windows as we thundered down Monterey. Some misguided girls and women tried to stand and shut the windows. Most were hurled back into their seats but a few doggedly managed it. Hats and caps streaked backwards in the bus if not caught mid flight. Shouts of encouragement soared to a crescendo with equally loud noises of reproach. Speedy was at Le Mans.

Suddenly, everyone became aware of a desperate, multiple bell-ringing and then, "JIVER! JIVER! STAP! STAP! Im **deaf**, nuh?!" There was a fiendish clacking of the conductress's coin on the railing, like Morse gone mad.

Speedy swung viciously into the curb, jammed on the brakes and screeched the tyres to a halt. The four boys on the rear bench shot forward off the seat, hung a minute in mid air and then, "Boof!"; they fell on the floor like rotten breadfruits. "Kunk!" The flying seat back was stopped by their cussing and swearing heads. Books, papers, school bags, the old woman's oranges and some people bounded or were sling shot to the front of the bus. Again people were grabbing hats; railings were gripped with knuckle-white power. The air hung thick with colourful "...Claht!!!!" and clouds of acrid smoke from burning rubber, engine and brakes. The kerosene...!

Besides the colourful reams of "...Claht!" there were a lot of other profane opinions. The bunch of us were stunned. The old lady was the only one unruffled. She had collared her stray kerosene tin and was looking around her with mild interest...not an unreasonable reaction...I guess...

"Look ere nuh Jiver, Me nuh know say if a you a go ome go feed fe mi five pickney-dem when Me dead! Me ave five pickney fe feed an Me a de ungle modder dem ave, so you jus carry me live which part Me a go, y'ear, Sah?! ...Ole rass!"

Buddha noted the scene, legs astride, arms akimbo. "See ere Lahd, Me nuh able fe dis man, yu know?! Look wha im do wid de public people-dem in a de govment bus!" Speedy didn't have any particular comment. All of it was just not part of the real world on the Grand Prix circuit.

Two people dashed off the bus behind me. "You is a FUckin eediot!" Yu nuh fit fe jive fowl! Gway man! Yu PUssy claht!"

A lady said, "Dem fe lock yu up! You is a public nuistance an a murderer! All like yu shoulda nevah ave licen becau Me sure say yu a go kill off de res o people-dem before yu reach dung a de rungabout."

Guffaws of shouting, cursing and laughter came through the windows as Speedy took off down the road oblivious and unimproved.

2

"De music sweet Baba!"

With the exception of the official green and white Jollies, every other kind of public transport had a chance to develop a personality and flavour special to a unit or group of vehicles.

The basic unit was made up of a threesome – the vehicle or *transpote*, the man who steers the bus or *jiver* and the collector of fares or *ductor* or *ductress*. The personalities of these units can be subtle or fairly shouted at you – as in the case of 'Sexy Tours'. The latter mini used to ply the route between Meadowbrook and somewhere around

Constant Spring. If the personality is subtle, it can take you a week or two of regular rides in order to discover the unit's true soul.

On the other hand, the Jollies were like so many hundred workers all wearing the same green and white uniform. The Duco job did not allow for individuality and the crews were on rosters so they were shuffled around. They had less potential for developing the indefinable 'je ne sais quoi'...trinity spirit, perhaps...in which a single member of a unit can represent the whole and yet be nothing without the other two. Except on the under utilised routes; like Route 67 which had small crew numbers; an individual Jolly had no trinity spirit whose aura could outdo that of the great entity – the JOS Company, Ltd. Society as a whole claimed the Jollies as its own.

One of the most obvious ways a team can project its personality is through what is written in and on the transpotes. The script can include the vehicles' names, thoughts for the day and general instructions and statements to the public. *(Look in the back of the book)* All are great forms of self-expression. The Jollies couldn't express personalities through writings because, on them, such writings are known as graffiti, so, if there were inscriptions, they weren't an expression of a specific owner or crew but of the members of the public who penned them. The Jollies were therefore the slates upon which society wrote – heavily used at election time.

Now the minis, vans and country buses – they are 'their own people'. Unlike Jollies, they dictate to society, not society to them – which is part of government's dying trial in attempting to regulate them. Similarly, it is the reason why a head or hand would be seriously damaged if a party with interest in a privately owned public transpote found anyone trying to express himself on any surface of his vehicle.

Then there is the sound system, which is very expressive of the unit's personality. Some vans and buses have none. Most of them have equipment ranging from pre-installed everyday systems to a battery of carefully selected tape decks, equalisers, radios, speakers and boom boxes. For the personal systems, brand names are only the best – Pioneer, JVC, Sony, and so on. Holes are bored for speakers or, in some cases, massive speaker boxes are discreetly located behind raised back seats, in the driver's well and other ingenious places. Most are played at ear splitting decibels and many are excessively distorted in the treble or bass range.

The standard music heard was dub and reggae or sexy pieces of soul like 'Sexual Healing'. Crews usually tend towards one school or other and sometimes it's dependent on mood.

Everybody had time for 'Public Eye' talk show, and one interesting example who worked the Stony Hill route never changed his station when 'LunchTime Concert' or 'Lunch Time Favourites' was on the air. One woman noted she, "...Doan know why im play dat music becau Me nuh understan it." That driver would have been interesting to meet, though.

Every so often a white pop star cuts a song that captures the nation at every level and everybody who owns a system records and plays it to death. These three were killers:-

'If You Want My Body'
'Oh Lord, It's Hard To Be Humble'
'Why Don't We All Just Get Stoned'.

The latter two were by the same artist. All have simple catchy melodies. The first two deal with sex appeal and the overblown ego – both very dear to the Jamaican heart – and the third is a social commentary on universal hard times.

A paint job can say a lot. Country buses are identified as a group both by structure and style of job. They are painted in bold horizontal swaths of colour. Nearly all have red somewhere. Navy blue is the next most common colour. Bottle green, light blue, yellow and orange are also known. Grey is very unusual, but has been seen. The buses are normally painted in at least three colour bands – body up to window area, window up to roof and finally the roof section.

'Buzz' was an exceptional piece of artistry and inspires detailed description. It was painted in bold undulating bands of brilliant red and white only. The tyres were white-walled and the outer edges of the rims were red. The name "Buzz" was painted on the front and bracketed by Mercury's wings in white. The Red Baron or Butch Stewart would have liked this one.

Like 'Buzz's' wings, all the country buses have signature emblems such as flowers, a five-point star, a heart, an insect, flags – including that of the US – racy stripes and endless other permutations and combinations, even Haitian-style pointillism.

And don't forget to check out Jamaican camouflage. It's an excellent record of the number and severity of the battles the vehicle has lived through. Grey, rust red and occasionally yellow; the beaten out body is prepared with these dull-coloured putties and primers which are left exposed on a temporary (read – permanent) basis; awaiting the next set of funds or skirmish. You get a sense of a work in progress.

Actually, the dimension of 'temporary permanency' is a very Jamaican paradigm. Einstein would have predicted such a situation since so many of us Jamaicans claim to be highly *conscious*. Look at the permanency of all those temporary and demonstration licence plates.

The country bus is also recognised by the standard roof rack. This rack is usually massively loaded to one third the height of the bus itself. Crocus bags and bankras stuffed to bursting with produce, crates of fowl, mounds of green bananas, straw-work, rose-apple strip and wiss baskets and the perennial packaging – banana trash – are piled up to the sky. Everything is skilfully and powerfully lashed down with stout rope. Still, it's miraculous that little, if anything, is ever lost – especially when you think of the horrendous list caused by the massive excess weight on top. Sometimes there is a well worn tarpaulin which is usually less well lashed down, particularly at its back end . When a bus with this shroud tears along country roads at night the wild flapping sounds like the cracking of a thousand whips and looks like some monstrous version of the headless horseman chasing poor Ichabod Crane. The careening bus is further announced by the well known blast or 'pama-pama' of the silver bugle- type horn over the driver's cabin. Most of these buses seem to be made by the same company.

New bus types have been introduced – the American type, which, I can tell you, is not going to make the grade; the Hispaniola-type covered pickup including one with the authentic, raucous Haitian pointillism I mentioned; the favourite Venezuelan 'Encaba-dem'; the Indian 'Tatas' which must represent some serious know-how about mass transportation under difficult conditions and, lastly, the Mercedes Benzs and Volvos with serious reputations for toughness and which should be able, if any can, to follow in the noble footsteps of Leyland.

Bus crews sometimes include a member who is easily recognisable by some feature or modus operandi, etc. The transportation unit is then identified by that person's trait – like 'De Coolie Gyal Bus', 'De Van Wi De Puss-eye Ductor', 'Speedy' and 'De Pickney Bus'.

3

Back To the Middle Passage

Usually, travelling on the privately owned public transport system of Jamaica was like a view back through the centuries to the Middle Passage. The slave packers might have picked up a few tricks from our bus and minibus crews...or maybe it's the other way round...

It didn't matter if the buses were regular or irregular, other than the rare former JOS bus – they were always rammed with passengers. Once or twice a JOS bus might pass up a stop if it could not hold another message.

One day, as we *bubbled* up Hope Road in a *ram-up* mini, I checked out how the mini was packed. There was a more or less central set of seats with a little space on one side and between seat rows. The front seat formed a spill barrier between the driver's section and the rest of the minibus behind him. In most of the Volkswagen minis, the solid back of the front, bench-style seat is a blessing. Without it people actually sat on top of each other in the front seat and under the elbow of the driver who might have a separate seat depending on the era of the bus's design. The spill barrier barely did its job though because the people in front usually had to suffer hot, often bad, breath exhaled down their necks. Sneezes and coughs might be sprayed and things like old bus tickets, coins and even the odd piece of chewing gum were often dropped down necks and bosoms. That day the packing was a senior piece of work. Each seat intended for 3 or 4, depending on passenger size, carried 4 or 5. The general rule is that when you could swear not another being could hold on the seat – he can. The space between the back of the front seat-cum-spill barrier and the first row of seating behind it was crammed with 4 people standing so that they were bent forward over the front seat: These people are the unfortunates who become criminals because they perform the normal bodily functions of breathing, sneezing and coughing.

Along the side of the bus where there is a small space meant to be a passageway for people boarding and leaving the bus, this too was packed. The people standing in this space formed parentheses arcing over the seated passengers. The laws of physics dictate that they absolutely must face inwards and hold on to the backs of seats, the exposed metal framework of the roof or both. Therefore, in a minibus, with heads and hands resting or pushing against it, the roof is usually black in spots and divided or pushed away from the supporting framework. Naturally, for a better grip on the framework, the roof lining is usually torn, with the stuffing hanging out, if it were there at all.

Under normal circumstances, there are two single rows of human parentheses, one on either side of the bus. That day, though, there were double rows – one set of parentheses arcing out so that their rear ends were neatly cupped, spoon fashion, by the concave stomachs of the outer set and the rears of the outer set stuck out through the bus windows. Eventually, Jamaican courts of law recognised this question with the formal charge of 'Body Protruding'. At first some of us thought it had something to do with indecent exposure.

I was on the edge of the seat nearest the door and a dread who couldn't find the standing space to make like a parenthesis, sat scrunched up beside me on the floor with his knees against his chest. His hands were laced together over his knees and his index fingers supported a scruffy but dignified chin. The locks were contained, not in a tam, but a bag – the newer, elongated or generally expanded version of the former. It was designed for serious locks and looked like a deflated wind sock. Thus philosophically posed, he stared straight ahead. His gaze didn't waver an inch.

Half-way up Hope Road, one of the passengers who formed part of an inner row parenthesis and who couldn't bear the cramped immobility anymore, swung round to face front. He was exactly in front of the seated dread so that his bottom was now directly in the dread's face. Without moving himself or his gaze one inch, the dread said levelly, "Come man, come, fix yu bottom good". The owner of the offending bottom tried to screw round – something like a crocodile trying to make a 180 degree turn – to see who had spoken, if it was to him, and what the offence really was. The bus load looked at the mad brown girl in the back (me), dying with laughter.

Okay now, that's one way of packing a minibus. In a lot of them, there is an extra seat added across the back where there used to be only storage space. It is always comfortable and since it's higher than the other seats, gives a bird's eye-view of everything.

Most of the popular Fords and Bedfords and the whole slew of Asian ones have seating that is staggered and there is usually some kind of crooked central aisle due to the staggering of the seats. Along the sides, some Ford and Bedford models have benches which face inwards so that there's a straight, wide aisle down the centre. This seat plan is not the original one – if there were any seats in the first place – because some are converted cargo vans. Crude, but ingenious welding and bolting jobs show up all over the place. In fact, whenever a particular seating plan looks unique or different, the original seats have probably been ripped out of the floor and new ones welded in in the interest of a more cost effective passenger pack.

In the staggered arrangement, people are randomly stuffed into whatever nook and cranny will hold them. On the buses with this arrangement, regular seats are filled first – no, crammed – and then the spaces are filled in with the standing passengers and...just when you think that's it...out come the upholstered planks of 2x4. What for, you ask? Why, make-shift seats of course! If the standing passengers don't block the way entirely – oh, sorry, such a thing would be impossible in Jamaican minibuses – these pieces of board are used to span the passage between seats and...voila! There is seating space for yet one more!

The crews on minibuses that have straight aisles use a method of passenger pack that looks something like well meshed machine cogs. This is the most effective format. On a well packed bus the resemblance to symmetry is so good that it looks almost like three human queues were plaited down the centre of the bus. Over-packing causes a loss of the semblance of symmetry, since people are then stuffed into the spaces between the plait. As with most things in the natural universe, there is an optimum.

We now turn specifically to the Japanese buses. As usual the Japanese either meet every need and/or beat everybody at their own game. Japanese buses have seats that flip down across the aisles so that the 2x4s become redundant. There are also seats above tyre cavities and seats that sit above the hot engine block. The Japanese have completely anticipated the exacting needs of the Jamaican minibus market. No minibus operator could more skilfully have engineered seating space.

The former Jollies and other kinds of big buses were packed alike no matter which company made them. Because the roof was high enough so that you didn't have to worry about banging your head, the full-size buses at their best pack were possibly more densely packed than minis. Poorly serviced routes were truly extraordinarily packed since whatever transport comes had to be taken – and it was usually a mini.

One evening, at about 6.30 p.m. at Half-way Tree, I was fed up with waiting and decided I was going to take a No. 30 bus if it killed me. Very near the truth but, funnily enough, I spent half of the trip in a good mood, marvelling. In a bad mood, there is no marvel – none – a human morass is a human morass.

So...like ants to sugar, we swarmed to the door of one of the bygone Jollies that seemed to inhale and exhale with the huge, collective breath of its dense cargo. At the back of this pushing, shoving throng, I watched as people squeezed in one by one. Each time one was swallowed up, you could look in through the windows and watch the peristaltic wave move down the solid column of standing passengers.

My turn. I made the long step from curb to first step at the bus door. Gutter water glinted darkly below me and it was risky business. People shoved from behind and it was difficult to pass the human wall on the bus steps.

Once you make it to the first step level of a really packed bus, the next entry requirement is the suppleness of a baby in the birth canal. You are 'en face', as they say in ballet – facing squarely in a given direction. Then, like the foetus making headway, from the hips down stays in the 'en face' position while the head and shoulders twist round to 'epaulement' position in ballet language – the line of least resistance in a small opening. You may then keep pushing and bring the lower body back to a position square with the upper body. This approach also looks like a living version of the people painted on Egyptian temple walls.

However, there are plenty more obstacles to overcome...the bankra in the passage, the gigantic woman's equally gigantic over-shoulder bag and the fear that the mad chewer behind will let fall his cud.

I turned one foot inwards and shoved it between a bankra and a hell-size pair of *sojier boot*. I wormed my other foot between two other *pair o foot*. Modern dancers should be trained in packed Jamaican buses – they would make great studios for learning body isolation techniques.

It's a good idea to rest your weight on the leg towards the rear of the bus because when first gear is hauled and the bus jerks forwards you must be able to stay standing. The thing is though, you can use your discretion. In my situation that afternoon, I was so tightly buffered on all sides that I didn't have control over my body parts, nor did I have to. As we lurched forward I couldn't have fallen if I'd tried. With my legs splayed around the bankra, one slightly turned in, I was bent forward and twisted away from the waist up to avoid being banged by a woman's huge 'Jetbag'.

Although the fluorescent lights were on, it was dark in my little corner of the world. The light barely filtered through the jungle canopy of heads, shoulder bags and upstretched arms. I cracked up and people stared at me again. It was past ridiculous and going to be a long haul from Halfway Tree to Stony Hill. All the same, I knew I'd soon be able to return at least my upper body to a normal position – people did get off the bus.

It was interesting that the bus kept stopping to load more passengers. Mark you, it wasn't by sight that I knew what was going on, but because I heard the muffled but loud command, "Come in a de bus, man! Yu nuh see de door kyaan shut?!" It finally rumbled shut.

This door closure business is a credit to those now keeping vigil over our public transport system. Formerly, door closure was a nuisance requiring drivers to remember to open and close doors and preventing many marginal passengers from free-loading.

I remembered something that happened up at Cavaliers. We were jammed tightly for the trip to Parks Road. A dread boarded the JOS and stuck himself in the open doorway.

The conductress informed him, "Y'ave fe come in mek de door shut."

"Mch!" was the reply.

"Me say de door ave fe shut – yu nuh ear?"

"Mch! Jive de bus, yaah!"

"De bus naah move till yu come in make de door shut!"

Now the passengers entered the fray. It was hot and sweaty and no time for foolishness.

"Come inside make de rass door shut man!" from an annoyed man.

Now the conductress: "Jiver, nuh go one place till dis ya man come in y'ear, Sah!"

The driver was getting disgruntled and revving up the bus, "Come Man, mek de oman do er job ow she know fe do it and mek people go bout dem business."

The passengers again: "Come in or cumoff Man, an stap hole up de bus!"

"All oonu rass, man, dis a public transpote an Me naah cumoff – oonu learn dat!"

The driver abruptly opened his cabin door, jumped down, slammed it shut and angrily sat on the roadside wall with his arms folded.

"Yu know someting, Sah?! De JOS operater-dem ave dem wuk fe do too, an it naah go do till it do right – so you learn dat one!"

Some passengers could still see humour, but mostly there were groans and, "Lahd Jeezas, watch ya now, is why dis ya man ave fe make so much chouble, eeh Sah?!" In public, this important Jamaican call on the Lord's strength means things are not yet so bad – some "...Claht!" and other niceties, would mean the worst.

The heat and cramping were getting to be a misery now. "TAKE YU RRRAAASS CLAHT OFF DE GOVMENT BUS, MAN" - Ah yes! Here, now, was breaking point – **"...Yu nuh ear de man naah jive yu go nowhe??!"**

"Oonu gwine mek me? Oonu ave right fe trow people off bus, dough?!"

"Naah, but Me ave right fe sidung ya whole day, so you stay deh," observed the driver.

The conductress: "A fe yu own good dem tell we say de door mus shut," she said to the general audience.

Again, "Mch!" was the reply.

"She a tell yu de lawful tings man, why yu kyaan ear, eeh?!" came from an older woman.

"An de ole bus ot to fart," murmured a woman fanning herself behind me.

"Jive de blood claht bus, Man, Me ungry!!!"

The driver said, "Yu ear, Sah? Yu a go up in a de bus mek people do dem job?"

The driver got off the wall and the offending dread seemed to know he had starred in his show long enough because he pushed up inside the bus. "Clack! Clack!" – the coin. "Chchch...Bash!" – the hydraulic door closing. The bus rocked forward at last.

An unnerving, squelching noise by my ear brought me back to the packed bus. There was a gum chewing maniac over my left shoulder. A tall boy chewed noisily and incessantly. He looked like a fool and it was not just a case of premonition, what followed was the obvious. "Plip!" The wet little pink wad flipped out of his mouth onto my shoulder, bounced off my forearm and dropped into the outside pocket of my bag. I grabbed it and hurled it out the window like all the vermin on earth were upon me. I gave the fool a withering look and muttered something. He naturally grinned back like a jackass.

Until that moment I'd been having a ball. Now, as I desperately tried to cleanse myself in the cramped surroundings, I was not happy.

4

'It Isn't Easy Being Green'*

In fact, I was damn' mad now. Why was I going through all this? My family had two cars. Why the hell wasn't I driving yet? Fine, so now I was among the masses...I wasn't black, I wasn't poor and I didn't smell. Where would it end? I wasn't a baby-modder's child either, like the hundreds filling the bus around me. Lord God! I looked around me – rabbits. Was my class really to blame for this? I didn't like the idea...worse still...I'd never really know. Maybe I was fate's victim just like them. The damn' trouble was, fate had me and a few others knowing too much blasted history and philosophy and wondering about how everybody manages in Jamaica. A heap of us end up feeling guilty, futile and/or confused.

When the left over dialectics and useless class junk stopped churning, I could see quite normally again that not every black person was poor and smelly – some were, but some weren't. Some leaned towards the standards of the developed world – kind of squeaky clean and artificially scented. Americans can get ridiculous with it though. But here's the rub – I'm short, so, on a bus, I often ended up with my nose in an undeodorised armpit. I know, bathing and deodorant is a culture thing, but they'd have made life easier for me on the bus. And the culturally implanted, follow-fashion spraying of 'Body Mist' and 'Elora' – over undeodorised butyric acid, mind you – Lord, man!

Once when I was in the Dominican Republic something had struck me, though. On the rush hour buses something was missing – then it hit me. No smell, or, nothing recognisably pungent. In Haiti I felt at home – same smell. Needless to say Dominicans think Haitians are smelly. As for me, I smell like a Jamaican – or a Haitian – if I don't bathe and deodorise.

"You is a Syrian or a Jew!"

I snapped back to the present and stared blankly at the man.

"Me know man, you is a Syrian!"

I saw the light. I didn't really look like the average passenger. I was brown and Latin-looking with not much jewelry and cool-coloured, loose cotton clothes. I had curly hair and no make up on.

I laughed. "You'd a frighten if yu know what a mongrel I am!"

He looked at me, shocked. Here was a decent-looking young woman calling herself a mongrel! Backgrounds dictate what you can call yourself. Had he looked like me, he certainly wouldn't have called himself a mongrel. He also would never refer to a soul as a 'madman' or a 'fool' either, except in vile argument. However, a friendly 'ole naygah' would be okay, but not from the likes of me.

I couldn't bother get into my not meaning to say that I was a stray animal, I just reeled off my very mixed background to him. His eyes opened wide.

"Um-um!" he said at my misfortune and I laughed. He was one of our black Jamaicans who could finally be openly proud of his African heritage. The man seemed genuinely sorry about my lack of pure, solid roots, whatever the race. With an unwavering stare he stated, "Well, Me's a Hafrican!"

I said, "No you're not. You're Jamaican jus like me."

"No, man."

"Oh yes, your ancestors might have been African and mine from all over, but we're born Jamaicans."

"Den ow come some Jamaica-man name Chiney an some name Indian?"

This was warming up. His logic was flawless. How comes black Jamaicans had no identity except their colour? There were Chinese and Indians, but something still didn't sit right. We were all Jamaicans! Why didn't we ever forget the stupid mother countries and get on with being Jamaican? I had an idea.

"You're Afro-Jamaican and the other ones, like Indians are Indo-Jamaicans and...," boy, I couldn't find any other neat labels for all other ethnic groups on the Rock, "...things that. You can't be African or Chinese or Jamaican if you're not born in those places." When Reagan came with his politricks, I learned the term 'Sino –'.

I was quite pleased with myself, but the man put a damper on it.

He smiled and said, "Den dem jus ha fe call yu Jamaican...dem nuh ave nuh name fe you."

"Well, I'm really Jamaican. I'm the complete mix-up of all the people here."

"Well, I-man prefer to know say I-man ave solid roots."

"Good for you," I said.

Hm! As Kermit sings, 'It Isn't Easy Being Green'. I was 'brown lady', 'Miss Chin', 'brown- skin' and Lord knows what else. As I looked up at the dense canopy of dark arms overhead I thought that whatever name they gave me, I was different, and the colour ratio was about right. I had one pair of the two or three lighter coloured pairs of arms in a bus crammed with at least 130 people.

*© *Children's Television Workshop*

5

Going Up...

Breakfas Stop

One summer, I worked in Tavern – Lawrence Tavern is too long a name for anybody – Unity, Border, Glengoffe, Parks Road and Above Rocks. At 7.30 a.m. sharp, you had to be at Constant Spring to catch the buses pulling out for all these areas in order to get to them at a respectable work-day hour. There was some special, unspoken rule about 7.30 a.m. departures. The buses were absolutely reliable and punctual at that hour. I can't explain that islandwide, early morning punctuality thing back then. It was odd.

I hopped into 'National Queen' and sat down. "B-A-L-T-I-M-O-R-E BURRURRUM...!" blared over the sound system. Damn it! Why couldn't I remember the stupid toilet paper to stick in my ears? The roar of the engine and the badly distorted sounds were ear-splitting. No one else was bothered and a few had their own private systems blaring other tapes or stations at full volume so the bus's sound system didn't interfere with their personal listening pleasure.

The mood was usually quite cheerful in the mornings, except for the face of the 'National Queen's' regular conductress. She was pretty but *er face sour*. We pulled into Stony Hill gas station for fuel – breakfast and gas. The conductress, her co- conductor and half the passengers got off for *bax juice an bun or biscuit*. Soon everything was ready and we were pulling out. The conductress had wandered across the square and was now fixing a baleful glare at the back of the moving bus. Er face was even more sour. As if it were being held in the tractor beam of her glare, the bus reversed to pick her up, and, moving like *she ave ook-worm*, climbed into the bus, flashing a deadly cut-eye at the driver's back. Her co-conductor, having read the nearly-left-behind scene perfectly, laughed out loud. She responded by plunking herself down in a pall of silence. There was absolutely no hope of mood improvement with her now.

I was sitting in the back seat with a slim, nice-looking girl. Fresh as the morning, she looked different from me who was dressed for field tramping. She was to my right and very close to me. All the same, the conductor who had been *smilin wid er* and flicking his tongue, squeezed himself between her and the woman on her right. The girl studiously **did not notice**...until the squeezing process accidentally pulled her filmy skirts high up her thigh. Equally surprised glances were exchanged between hawk and chicken and before anyone could move, with a dashing gesture which I couldn't decide to be mannerly or not, the conductor deftly pulled down her skirts with an urbane smile. The young lady resumed eyes-front while everyone sitting around them hid smiles.

It wasn't over yet. The conductor smiled snakishly at the girl's profile and loudly whispered, "My name is Mout-water!" The girl kissed her teeth and turned up her nose. Everyone who had heard, and the offender, broke into laughter but he soon had to leave his dalliance to attend to his duties.

A couple of days later I discovered his 'real' name (sure as anything he was legally named something else) was Rusty. Rusty was an attractive man – very short hair, smooth chocolate skin, a really gorgeous body and the most unique – almost oriental – eyes I'd seen for a while. He noticed me because, once again, I looked different. When he was being kindly and attentive, I had no problem with his show of gentlemanliness, but if he got on the *facety* side, I was *facety back to im* and he stopped his foolishness. We developed a mutual respect.

Some mornings later, on the bus that goes round to Harker's Hall, a young dread began chatting me up.

"What yu name? Yu need company dahlin?" ...and on and on.

I replied, "Look, if yu wan talk to me, talk, but doan come wid nuh foolishness."

"I-man not comin wid nuh foolishness, I-man doan talk foolishness." He was put out.

"Well anyway...I'll talk to yu if yu treat me like I have brains too."

With the wind completely out of his sails and stupid, leering attitude gone, the question was, "What yu doin rung ere den?"

"I came to look after what mothers and babies eat," I explained. Now there were slightly rash, but sincere, offers of help and accompaniment or protection and so on, and most of all, genuine interest in my work. When Olive Lewin had talked to us in 2nd Form, I'd got the message – speak to people like they are your equals and watch the results.

A little later I hopped off the bus at Zion bridge and went across the road to wait for a work-mate. I began chatting to a little old man who was sitting in the sun.

"When they goin' finish the bridge, Suh?"

"Hm! Dat deh bridge buil an buil an all now it kyaan buil yet! Is nuh de politrician-dem! An after it buil, yu know, it kyaan good like de ole one deh, yu know. Dat deh bridge flood out an flood out an till a tan. A dem politrician same one come rung ere come ot up de area an tun de whole o de young bwoy-dem fool. Dem doan ave no respec..." I followed his gaze to a group of rudie boys by the construction shelter at the bridge. "...Wid dem long air an foo-foo talk..."I-man Dread"...an all dem chupidness. Yu jus mek one o dem come fas wid me y' ear Sah an Me jus gi im one chop!" he said brandishing his machete like no 'little old man'.

There were about eight young loafers at the construction site across the road and they called to me. They'd been doing this since I'd come off the bus. Some of the sounds were like those you'd hear in a snake pit. I took them on and went over. Dead silence – called their bluff. "What yu want me for?" Fidgeting, some giggling and then, "Why yu doan come out o de sunhot an wait ere-so in de shade?" came from one of them.

"No! I wan to talk to de ole man." It had happened again. Women just could not leave the victim role without causing consternation. Well, I had and the impression left was obvious. I trotted back to the old man.

On another early morning in the country it was, as nearly always, bright and clear. The sun would soon be brilliantly hot but the morning air was chilly as usual. At this hour of the day, the ride through Golden Spring, along the valley floor by Temple Hall and up to Unity and Border was good for your soul and so was the one to Parks Road and Glengoffe.

At the regular point on our route, we sank into the cool, muffling, Temple Hall mist. Driving up out of it was like climbing into a magic world. Sounds again became sharp and clear as the view. Now we were looking out over snow fields of hanging cloud. Sunshafts just touched them and the tallest trees poked through, angel hair mist floating around their branches. Minutes later, the new heat was melting small holes in the vapour and islands of green jungle appeared in a white sea. Oriental water colours came to mind... Sunlight splashed the sleeping backs of the suddenly bright, bamboo-tufted mountains.

Cool air blessedly rushed through the windows of the bus now crammed with Oberlin High Schoolers. This drive had a drawback. It was the one on which I was first, and most often afterwards, aware of the helplessly sick, lurching feeling that can overcome you inside a packed bus as it winds around Jamaica's serpentine roads. It turned corners and my imagination ran riot with the ebb and flow of adrenaline in my gut... It would be a God-almighty, crushing and breaking of bones and bodies, hopelessly trapped by their own weight. You couldn't do anything to stop the precarious feeling of the weighted JOS... Nothing at all!

When you got off at the Glengoffe square in the morning, you were really in a rainforest clearing. The cocoa tree groves alongside the road were thick with mist and dripping with dew. The sound of drops on the mat of fallen leaves was like an isolated rain shower bounded by the road. Sunshine slanted in among the trees and hit the rich reds, russets, oranges and golds of the ripe pods and dead leaves. Heavy mist was usually a good sign that it would be a blistering day. Lack of it in the morning usually meant overcast or rain later on. Over the dewfall was the woodpecker's raucous cry or drumming in the distance.

6

And Coming Down...

Coming down out of the hills in the afternoons, the mood in the buses was either sombre or riotous. Crisp golden afternoons and Fridays usually went with the good mood. Rain, heat, Wednesdays, etc., were predictors of weariness and short tempers.

It was a rainy 3.00 p.m. Route 31 JOS was lumbering to the gates of Oberlin High on its way down the mountain. The conductress stood up to do battle. "Um-hm! Watch ere now!", she said ominously under her breath. It was clear why she was bracing for an onslaught.

Below the bus windows was a sea of bobbing umbrellas, plastic bags, newspapers, school bags, one banana leaf and other kinds of rain gear, makeshift and standard. The rain fell greyly on them all...and they converged on the door. Above the shouting, chattering, laughing and general mob racket, could be heard a raised voice in the wilderness.

"Oonu mek big people come firs!" Adults went first. There is something about being thrown together with children that causes Jamaican *big people* to become models of discipline and comportment for fear they be likened to or compared *wid de pickney-dem*. When there are no pickney around, the behavioural reversion is astounding.

Then – "Awright, all de pig an og-dem come now, das right, pig an og time, now!" Unfortunately, this attempt at reverse psychology directed at the youth failed. The pigs and hogs barrelled in through the door.

"Whe yu 10-cent deh?"

"Oo payin fe yu?"

"Whe de ticket Me jus done gi yu?"

"Mchch, jus dress down gi people room, y'ear. Me say shub down an small-up yuself!"

"Ow much o yu comin in on de one ten-cent?"

"Awright, oo doan pay as yet?"

"Is whe im gone eeh, Sah? Yu tink I doan see yu, nuh? Come out from under de seat yu likkle culprit yu!"

"But Jeezas, oonu doan ave **no** manners!"

"Whe de ten cents she jus gi yu? Mch...! Me say a whe de fare fe er?

"Is dat dem do all de while yu know...take de fare from de likkle one-dem, tell dem say dem a pay fe dem an den push de money in a fe **dem** pocket! I shoulda stap de bus right ere-so an make oonu fine oonu way ome. Come in ya come do dat one more time an see wha Me do wid yu... Hm! Oonu take dis ting fe joke now..."

Another mid-week afternoon coming down, I caught a lovely empty bus and sat down with pleasure. I was staring out the window thinking. I loved empty JOS buses better than any other kind - the newer screwdriver industry ones particularly. When they were empty, they gave you a complete feeling of space and cleanliness and the bone-shaking rattling of every nut, bolt and window added to the cavernous feeling. There was also no driver immune to the charms of an empty Jolly either. They careened the buses at an imaginary Paris-Dakar. This only added to the massive bumping and jolting of everything and all the few bodies inside. It was great, like a weird and wonderful massage, every limb going to a different tempo.

An empty-bus ride is a time capsule. You can't do anything but travel, observe and think. You certainly can't read unless you want to go cross-eyed or get nauseous or both. There's lots of space and time for thought. I thought...about my work in the country.

The violins whined out the social dialectics in my head again and I wondered about teaching 'oppressed people' to eat right. The politicians were really trumpeting that 'oppressed people' business now. I sensed my work was really on the wrong jag. Just like the residents of upper St. Andrew, the 'oppressed people' in my project treated food and shelter as incidental to life, and the car and TV as the real goals. They had latched onto Upper St. Andrew values, but were now being told that good nutrition should come first...which did not go over big. Was I doing social penance because of the damn' conscience nagging? No, I thought I was lucky and I wanted to give something back. At least it wasn't a rank charity affair, although the whole business was run like one. It would have been better with a more business-like and consumer oriented approach. What was the 'oppressed people's' own stake in bettering their lives?

Mch...chuh fart! As usual, 'the ever decreasing circle till you...' Hmm! Later for that...

Suddenly, I noticed a minor commotion beside me. Two school boys were seated behind an otahiti apple lady. She had her bankra firmly jammed and stabilised between wide open legs. Her frock was stretched to its limits. The basket was heavy with ruby-coloured fruit carefully packed in banana trash.

"Ey, Miss James, yu no member me?" The boys were laughing and up to something. The woman kissed her teeth and *made up er face.*

"Is you dat Miss James?! Is dis long time Me nuh see yu. Tun rung mek a see yu sweet face again."

More kissing of teeth, "Yu gwaan y'ear," she advised with a face that was anything but sweet.

The boys looked at each other knowingly. One piped up, "Oh Lahd, .Miss James! Me did know say is you! Is ungle you talk sweet so! Come labbrish wid me wha yu do wid yuself all dese long ears!"

Her eyes looked for Heaven's strength. "Me say fe lef people an go mine oonu own business an llow dem fe mine fe-dem own, tch!" she intoned over her shoulder, profile to the young gallants.

Perseverance had won many a battle and the boys pressed on. "Is you tek yu sof han pick dem lovely rosy apple, nuh Ma? Look pon dem, not a one bruise nor mash. An look ow dem pack nice an sof. Plenty man nuh ave nuh bed stay so."

The woman's back stiffened a fraction. The boys grinned. Score one. She hadn't looked at them once, probably because if she had, she'd have been lost. I had seen something flicker around the corner of her mouth. All eyes were riveted on the scene, everyone in the bus was now mentally placing bets on the outcome. Most were smiling and chuckling.

"Is apple oonu want, nuh?" Attack was the best method of defense. "Well, oonu naah get none! Oonu too out o order!"

"Oh Lahd, Ma, yu wouldn share likkle bit wid yu long los frien-dem? If Me did ave ungle likkle bit, yu know say Me'd a share it like de poor man in a de chuch an gi yu de alf o it, even aldough say is all Me did ave in dis worl!"

Brilliant! She smiled. Although the boys didn't see it, her long silence told them yet another point had been scored.

"Oh Ma, look ya!" one pleaded. "De drive soon done an yu nuh even talk to we make we know say ow yu dah do!"

Oh my! This woman was hard, mi son! We were nearly at Constant Spring and she really wasn't going to give in and give them an apple each. The bus stopped at Manor Park and the boys stood up to leave. They were still in good spirits. Then the woman stood up too. The boys looked at each other, eyebrows raised. With a great and chivalrous flourish they stepped back to let her pass. Struggling with the weight of her fruit, the woman waddled past the boys, face stony, eyes front.

"Mek we carry it fe yu, nuh Ma?" They trotted off the bus after her. Just on the curb she turned and, without expression, fished in the bankra and flung the boys two apples. Their faces lit up. The conductor was jubilant. He laughed and passed on the good news, "She gi dem it! She gi dem it!" Everybody was laughing, "What a set o pickney dough, eeh Sah? Dem good dough, dem work ard fe it!"

7

On A Moully Afternoon...

On another afternoon it was hot and *moully* and we'd been waiting at least an hour and forty-five minutes at Tavern. Everybody was feeling nasty. Flies were everywhere. It was mango season and there was a little butcher shop just up the road from the bus stop. The smell of unrefrigerated raw meat, blood and organs was overpowering in the heat, nothing rotten, just raw butchery. The grinning perpetrator, blood- spattered from head to toe, walked up and down through the square. The butcher's sanitary 'whites' weren't that condition or colour anymore and the rubber boots were caked with *dread* looking red mud. The gutter water had a rosy tinge.

Hands, books, bags, hats, paper – everything was flapping at flies. I looked down to swat one off my chest. It wasn't one, but two – mating right there on my blouse! They, of course, needed more encouragement than usual to go elsewhere with their business.

"Mmmmph, Lord!", I rolled my eyes. Too much in one day, man! Then I really bawled out laughing. In a grubby bucket on the ground beside me was the head of a scalped cow, eyes and nostrils flaring up at me. Sensory overload now! The tongue and teeth still had the ruminants' greenish tinge. Flies buzzed around and pitched. A death mask, very recently butchered! Dante's Inferno was definitely getting a run for its money today.

The little man in the restaurant directly behind me offered me a stool to sit on. The bus stop sign was planted in the sidewalk so that it almost bisected the entrance to his shop. I thanked him and sat just inside the doorway. Waiting on the damn' bus would be my dying trial!

A strong, friendly looking man walked up to the wiry little woman with the cow-head. She was in brown with a brown wool cap. Two holes were cut in her *ole booga so dat de likkle toe-dem wouldn burn er.*

55

"What yu sellin today, Miss Azel?"

"Me a go dung a Waterhouse Lane wid it, mi dear Sah!"

"Hm! Yu nuh easy at all. Not even man a go deh now!"

"Lahd mi dear, Me know ow it stay, but man ave fe eat, nuh?! Sake o de voilence, whole eap o people-dem kyaan come out fe buy dem bickle an Me a mek a good money a sell in deh."

"Awright Ma, Me wi see yu!"

"Take care Mas Andy."

He walked into the eating place and began chatting with the little owner.

"Hm! Me nuh go a tung fe joke dem time now, yu know, Massa! De less Me go a dem place deh de better. An when Me go, is bare ole clothes Me wear becau anyow yu put on deestent clothes go deh, de bad boy-dem tek yu mek target. Mek dem tear off de ole shirt off mi back, but dem naah go way wid fe mi new one-dem. No Sah, not even police safe down deh now! De rudie-dem a tek dem mek poppy show! An Me shub my money in a fe mi shoes bottom!"

"So Me ear, Sah. What yu want? Cornmeal puddn?"

"Eehi. Gimme two o dat an a bax juice, nuh."

Eating heartily, mouth full of pudding and juice, Mas Andy carried on his slightly onesided conversation.

"No Sah, Me nuh coward. If man back me up, **Me** carry **my** knife an Me wi fight. But Me nuh eediot neider; Me naah go look worries, y'ear Sah. Me all ear some o dem say yu nuh fe wear orange nor green dung deh, mek dem shoot yu fe PNP or Labourite".

"So Me ear, Sah, so Me ear."

At this stage I frankly didn't care who else was seated and who not, I thanked God I was. The little brown lady was shifting from foot to foot now.

"Is wha mek wid dis ole bus, eeh Sah? Lahd Jeezas man, Me ave mi business fe go bout, an watch ya, one o'clock ketch me up ya. Mchch...haaaaiiii, Sah! An when dem late so yu know, dem take yu dash yu way over de illside de way ow dem fly go down. An dem pack-up too, yu know."

However, a *pack-up* JOS or big bus was much better than a mini as the drivers of the small ones "...Shouldn even drive fowl an wan kill off de people-dem, de way ow dem reckless!"

I hoped to God the cowhead lady would stay far with her stinking meat. The smell of blood was going to fill up the whole bus.

School children were making their usual ruckus to pass the time, chasing each other all over the square and having various adults and drivers shout at them to "...Move demself from out o de road!"

Chaos! And though several men *smile wid me* and offered me rides, I declined, not much trusting either men or rides. God, man! I just wanted to get home!

The bus finally hurtled to the stop. It was *pack-up*. I nearly cried. However, with the best of the shovers and borers, I intended to get a seat on that bus!

The bus heaved off and Miss Hazel wrestled with her cow-head bucket and pans of offal in the cramped passage. People avoided her as best they could and even though, Lord be praised, she wasn't beside me, the bus was hot, stinking and stifling...and I stood all the way home...

8

& On A Brilliant Afternoon

On one of those fantastic golden Friday afternoons that make you think, "Evenin' time…",* the driver clearly had the fever too. He was tearing down the hill, skilled reflexes razor sharp on the corners and inclines. It was 6.00 p.m. on the home run and there was a sparkling mood. The sound system blared 'Drunkin' Masta' and other toe-tapping musical excitement like 'Supersition' by Stevie Wonder. JBC was in the mood too. Chatter, laughter and jokes ricocheted around the bus. Life was in love with itself! That Jewish kick-over-the- traces song, 'Lachaim!', was the only thing left for JBC to play that afternoon and I must have smiled – no, grinned – all the way down to Constant Spring.

Rusty was in fine form, mischievous and charming as the devil. A gallantry performed here and a rudeness there. He was up and down the crowded aisle, slipping in and out with a now-you-see-me-now-you-don't technique that was extraordinary. This was the animal in his element, the goat on the mountainside. The bus's swerving and gear hauling told him nothing; his comings and goings were unaffected. A champion of his ilk, he might have stabilised himself with a hand rail once. To his type, a careening bus was solid ground. Money was collected and change returned without pause. Then, as if taken by an uncontrollable urge to express himself, Rusty dashed for the door and grinning from ear to ear, swung wildly from it with the sheer joy of life which, from my point of view, looked soon to be snuffed out. He laughed and whooped like an avenging Hun at the old war game of peg-o-the-tent. He crouched down and lashed an imaginary steed. Terrain flashed past dizzyingly. Suddenly, he made a death defying swoop forward out of the door – lunging with the invisible lance. His outer arm swung round in a full arc and the inner arm went free of anything inside the bus. "Jeeesus!" escaped me. Some people watching

Rusty's antics turned, wondering what my outburst was about. With consummate grace and skill Rusty had grabbed hold of the bus door at the last minute and was hanging on again.

It's funny how everyone always has words of caution for girls and some women about being careful, holding on, etc. For example, "Hole on baby, mine yu drop!" but not a God's soul would even vaguely think of cautioning Rusty or any of his kind.

Starting up the Stony Hill slope from the Temple Hall valley, Rusty, hanging out the door, shouted, "WWWWOOOOYYYY! IM DROP! HEH HAAAYYY! WATCH DEH, NUH!" All heads spun backwards and stuck out of windows and doors. About ten people piled over Rusty to get a better look. By rights he should have *dropped* too.

I could just see a man racing to catch the bus. I was dazed. Rusty banged the bus side to signal the driver to slow down and he who had fallen by the wayside leapt in through the bus door wiping a bleeding forehead. He was met with riotous laughter and resounding claps on the back. He smiled his acknowledgement. The bus side was banged again and the driver picked up speed.

It could have been a case of hopping the bus and missing or falling out of the front of the bus or, most likely, falling off the back after hitching a potential free ride. It was unlikely he paid anything after the incident, though.

Imagination and fear are cultural mindsets so here in Jamaica, life and limb are not more important than catching a bus. Hard life probably makes you reckless and, whatever happens, be it accident or near death, "Yu jus ha fe love it!" or "...Hug it up!"

We went on home in the fading sunlight, the mood still high. Shadows were very long now, but sharp in the clear air. "Evenin' time..." floated over me again as I stared out the bus windows at a crystal sky with its lone evening star. The striking copper and green of star-apple leaves shimmered in the last rays. Could the woman who had written the tune for that song really have been English? Maybe just English parents... Whatever... She was more Jamaican than plenty of us born here!

Copyright – Louise Bennett-Coverly & Barbara Ferland

THE PASSENGERS

9

Terror! That's what I felt when I first became an unaccompanied passenger on JOS.

Eleven years old and my father had condemned us to take the bus! We, his children, should learn to use public transport and be independent. After all, thousands of Jamaican children took the bus to school every day. We were spoiled. Mummy saw to it that we got up, got dressed, got to school. Enough of that rubbish...

"We should just leave you to do all that by yourselves and then see what would happen!"

Very likely what happens in thousands of other homes – we'd have been instantly absent.

Dad would sometimes watch us through the window to see we were off on the bus without any problems. If we were late because we dawdled and missed the bus, we'd learn because we'd have to face the terrible consequences of walking into Sister's or Father's class, late. Sometimes, however, they gave in and chauffeured us, all the while making the required parental noises of chastisement.

Through all the confusion clouding my introduction to Jamaican public transport, I set out on a larger journey that kept my parents under nail-biting stress during Jamaica's 'fighting years', 1975-1980. This diary is the result. I took the inch, ran the mile and haven't been seen as a transportation dependent since.

Anyway, there came the day that I had to pack myself onto the bus alone for the first time. Mummy dropped me to school. My uniform, funnily enough, had been dirty so I had gone to school in 'normal' clothes, a blue and white, pleated shift with front pockets that buckled up. In First Form, I didn't know about the "The Ides of March" and things like that, but that was no excuse, I had ignored a sign. On top of it, Diane, the big girl who lived next door, and who faithfully accompanied us on every one and one-half mile long bus trip to school, was now telling me she couldn't make it that day! Lord God...I couldn't even phone Grandpa and tell him to rescue me! Sister had locked up the office and gone!

Woe was me. Fear stuck in my throat like a lump of hot yam.

Well...This was it. I pulled the elastic band of my straw hat into place under my chin. I felt the purple and white ribbon tail at the back tickling my neck. The badge stood out on the front and "VIRTUS ET VERITAS" would shine forth that day.

Firmly, but slowly, I set off up Old Hope Road, my clammy hand clutching my minigrip school bag. I was so out of it I didn't even remember the all boys' school up the road on the right where khaki-dressed hooligans and Zulus – that's what Grandpa said they were – waited for prey with spears and arrows of wild, rude jeering. How..."Yu smiley dis an yu ugly dat," and on and on about, "Sweet biscuit an mash-up crackers..." It was unbearable. It never bothered Diane though, or anybody who never took them on.

The bus shelter was coming closer.

I moaned. If only I could have called home. Surely I could find a telephone somewhere. It wasn't fair. How, God, could I reach up and pull the bell cord...and what if I didn't or the driver didn't hear it and shot past my stop? One driver used to do it a lot. Suppose he let me off at the next stop...because he'd flown past mine? It was too much to bear. And if I went for broke and tried it and it did go wrong? Could I, maybe, fight the two hundred yards back up Monterey to my stop and save myself from the unbelievable embarrassment of looking like I hadn't managed to get off at my own stop? The thing was, a lot of people on the bus knew where my real stop was...

No! I would pull that bell string *doan care* what... But everybody in the whole bus would be watching my hand reach up for the cord. I couldn't stand the shame. And when to pull it? A terrifying decision; too early and I'd look over anxious and new, too late and I'd be lost – shot past the stop!

"Mchchchch!" I kissed my teeth. So what if, "Thououououousands of other children took the bus every day..." – yeah, yeah! I could hear Dad - "...Younger than you, and alone". I didn't care, I was in terror.

"Mch!" I sulked...and Diane would have told me when to pull the cord or do it herself. She always did it so easily. By now it was normal for her and she didn't care about doing it.

"Mch!" I thought...at first my parents and the whole of Hope Pastures had gone on so badly about Route 67...how it would bring noise and wake up people at 5.30 in the morning and cause trampled banks and hedges with garbage allover the place and bring all kinds of butus into the area.

Well actually, the first year was kind of rough on my parents. For at least that time, they stopped using an alarm clock because 5:30 a.m. was announced by the arrival of Jolly JOS outside their bedroom window. They were suffocated as they lay, in stinking diesel fumes from the idling and gunning of engines. Curse the tropical, once romantic, floor to ceiling louvre walls and God bless the saving grace of the high privet hedge.

And if that weren't a rude enough awakening; there was a male regular by whose seismic and productive sinus clearings you could set your watch to within plus or minus 5 minutes of 6:00 a.m.

The neighbourhood had plotted and schemed together and one night, people met noisily like a party, at our house. Mr. Kirton, the then general manager, would be petitioned. Other routes and solutions would be suggested to him. They were really carrying on about the invasion of Jolly JOS into their neighbourhood. I even saw them with maps and things. The supernova burned to a white dwarf, but before the burn out, the heat passed even to the children.

One afternoon there was a showdown that was bound to happen. The regular game of street football was in progress. The gateways of the Smiths and the Jones facing each other from opposite sides of our avenue formed the goals. The ball ran out from under the hedge and into the path of a rumbling, reversing Jolly. The bus humped over something and – P O W !! – the exploded pieces flew every which way to a chorus of **"Raaahtid!" "Jeesum Peace!" "Yu hear dat!"**

Colin's ready mind was at work almost before the sorry pieces of ball came down... Revenge... His wiry figure vanished into his house and he came back laughing like the little devil he was. In his hand was a match box that sounded like a rattler's tail – naturally, the boy also happened to own a real tail. The box was filled with long tacks. He waited to hear the engine roar to life and then tore out through his gate. He and his henchmen stooped at the hated bus's big back wheel and then everybody scattered seconds later as it began to roll away. It was just getting away around the corner when..."Doom-doom, doom-doom..." Mission accomplished; the beast was hit! The ignorant bus had a flat! Shouts of laughter split the air.

I guess Dad and our neighbours had been practical people and, since they couldn't beat 'em, we were sent to join 'em. The children of all those militant parents were regularly travelling with the Jamaica Omnibus Service.

I think I remember being sick with relief. At the crucial moment of decision-turned-action...somebody else dinged the bell. I sank down in cold sweat. I was off the hook. God was on my side the day of my first solo trip. A few seconds later, I tumbled through the bus door and onto solid ground. I was home free, not the slightest embarrassment. I'd done it! It would get easier now.

I didn't need Diane anymore.

10

It Takes All Kinds...

The passenger *collideoscope* is really what makes public transport. It includes skaters, madmen, preachers, sellers, etc. – and the average commuter.

The skater is hair-raising to watch. The first time I saw one, I was in a mini doing about 45 m.p.h. up Hope Road. Another minibus tore past us – 60 m.p.h. at least – and I did a double take. My God! There was a man on skates hanging onto the back of the other bus. His open shirt snapped and whipped behind him heightening the dare-devilry. He was lithe and taut looking and absolutely at home in his situation. It was horrifying. But that was nothing, man! The overtaking mini veered sharply in front of us followed carelessly by its human caboose. It went close to the sidewalk and the man let go the bus back and, mind bogglingly, jumped the curb at 60 m.p.h....and just kept on going down the length of Jamaica House's sidewalk. A free agent, he neatly negotiated the break at the entrance to the driveway. Only when his momentum was dying did he fail to roll along exactly beside our mini which was still doing 45 m.p.h. Only one or two other passengers saw any reason to remark on the matter.

Jamaicans either react or don't. There is little in-between. A madman proved this. If possible, he was the saddest, weirdest thing I've seen on our streets. There was a ghastly symbolism about him - something like a Latin-American surrealist's character. Where it could be seen through crusts of black filth built up over months, he had honey- gold skin from the hours spent shirtless in the sun. Blond, low cropped afro hair made him look like a St. Elizabeth Red. His front and rear ends were obviously free under the equally filthy, torn, cut-off,bold, black and white checkered pants. His bare feet were splayed and calloused. His head was mostly covered with an executioner's hood, stark black, and around his neck hung a ragged hemp noose. Whichever way you looked at it – he was victim and executioner at the same time, acting out insanity's cyclic trap.

The man jumped the bus and hung on at the bus door windows which had long since had their glasses broken out. The conductress looked at this newest nuisance in her life, raised her eyes to heaven and sat down, her back to the scene.

"But is why Me ave fe put up wid all dem crosses, Lahd?"

A couple of chuckles at the conductress's troubles and now and then a look out the window. The bus rolled along.

As we came to the turn-off at Mannings Hill Road, we passed a bar by a supermarket. Two men leaned against the wall. As if struck by lightning at least, they shot off the wall and rushed half-way into the street. Doubling over with laughter at the madman, they shouted, "HU-RASS, WATCH DEH! WATCH DEH! LOOK DEH, NUH! LOOK DEH...! To bumbo!" They kept dancing about gleefully in the middle of the road until I couldn't see them anymore.

The madman was so intent on where he was going. I could see his eyes narrowed against the wind. He finally jumped off. The conductress chuckled and shook her head.

It doesn't have to be Sunday for the appearance of the self-styled missionary. These travelling evangelists, both men and women, seem to surface mostly in the morning as opposed to another kind that stakes out the bus terminus in the evening. I don't remember having seen more than one of the travelling kind on my way home at nights.

Their voices are loud, penetrating and usually nothing like their speaking voices. They go on interminably about fire and brimstone and also the fact that placing yourself entirely in Jesus's hands results in complete solution of your problems. Most of the preachers can quote chapter and verse. No one appears to notice. The audience is all blank-faced but for the rare head accepting the Truth with a rhythmic nodding.

Apart from empty-bus rides, which relaxed me and gave me time to think, Sundays and early mornings were the times I noticed how good-looking Jamaicans can be, probably because they were clean and fresh for the day. Even though many are as clean and tidy as possible, there is now a new school of young men that believes that although you must still *bade-off*, you must put on the most ragged, terrible, *dread*-looking clothes possible. Uncared locks, uncombed hair, bottle-green *darkers*, *gun-mout* pants cut off at the knees, ankle boots and T-shirts or merino-style ganzies are 'style'. There was also a style of elaborate hole patterns cut into T-shirts. I saw the style in the Dominican Republic before it got here.

Once, I was looking down the aisle at a man's forearm. It wore a gold watch and was dark brown, smooth and sinewy – couldn't tell the age. The hand was big and strong, had seen much service. It lay quietly on a solid well-developed thigh and the whole impression was one of quiet power. Nothing to prove, the strength was obvious. The arm disappeared into a pale pink and white pin-stripe, cotton short-sleeve shirt. Broad shoulders. Lots of West Indian men's arms are beautiful. They look like ideal sculpture in dark hardwoods. Some are not hairy people and the dark skin has a special sheen that shows off the muscles. Quite a few have long fingers and nail bases.

The man in the pink shirt was handsome too. He had a big nose with wide nostrils and a wide mouth with lips that were broad but didn't protrude to break the hardness of his profile. The face had deep-set eyes, high cheek bones and not a hint of slackness or jowls. The eyes and lines of the well scrubbed and shaved face told a story of quiet resolve before life's trials. He'd probably seen a lot and I had a sense that he might have worked abroad as a farm or construction worker.

The man in the pink shirt was a reminder that names and ages rarely crossed my mind while looking around me on the bus. Yet, I might wonder and ask about names and ages of people like TV announcers or someone at a party maybe... It really didn't matter at all, even if I was good at guessing ages;but with these travellers, only twice in fourteen years had I wondered about age and, both times, nothing could be pin-pointed. I could only figure in a ten- to twelve-year range... Why? I looked around me harder. There was a strong feeling that few of them looked their ages. From behind they looked old beyond their years or so young that only when they turned around did their faces give clues to the truth. The hard life either destroyed their bodies or created an eternally youthful attitude to the challenge.

11

Family Life Education

Other things could fool you about their ages too.

Yes, she could be fourteen or maybe twenty-two. She was in charge of either four younger brothers and sisters or four children aged six months to three years. Old women, eighty years old, had serene faces and barely plump bodies and looked sixty. Forty-year olds had bruised and whitlowed hands, bent backs, round shoulders, dead eyes and looked like the grave would have been welcome or they were so fat they looked fifty-five.

The men were mysterious too since the majority were mostly relieved of the 'extra burden' of raising children, while at the same time, some took to alcohol and brawling in or out of the home.

Although beaten women are numerous, I never noticed one while on the bus. Had there been any, they certainly wouldn't have made it public knowledge, unlike a smallish, gentle, rather hen-pecked looking man I once found at the Stony Hill stop. He was sadly complaining to a large, strong looking woman that his girl had run out on him for the third time. He was instructed to "...Lef er an gwaan becau she wan stone since she nuh know good tings when she ave it!" He sat on the market steps, his chin in his hands. He was just average size but in his confusion looked very small. His clothes were immaculate and his sparkling white crepes were as neatly appointed as his well tucked in shirt. I had the feeling he was entirely to blame for his own neatness.

The advice to "...Go look deestent oman an nuh worry tek up wid nuh more tegereg..." ran on parallel to "...An all ow me did try mi bes wid er..."

Looking at him was so hurtful, but you'd never have a chance to casually know about the other side of the coin in society, much less see and feel for her as with this little man. There was 'no such woman' because had she publicised her problem, she would have got some *kick an tump* or the man would simply have brought a girlfriend right into the home – maybe even kicked the original partner out.

They were rare creatures, but the battered men certainly could look for public sympathy – like this other male domestic casualty who made my eyes water imagining the pain. He was sitting in the back of a bus coming down from Stony Hill – makes you wonder about Stony Hill women, eh – and was obviously on pain killers. One deeply tinted plaster covered the upper part of a diagonal gash slanting down, right to left, over the right brow. Running across the left side of his face was another plaster, puffed out with still seeping blood and lymph. The upper edge of this was hanging away from the same wound which now continued its way down across his nose-bridge; dangerously close to the left eye; near to its inner corner and tender lower lid. I blinked a lot. The lower, most brutal part of the gash tore on down just below the left cheek bone and peeped from behind the plaster. It was ragged and stitched and was obviously caused by a down stroke when she smashed the bottle across his face for telling her "...To stop walk street a night time". I rubbed my eyes. He might have been blinded in an instant.

The men in his audience were loudly holding forth about "...Wha dem woulda do wid a oman like she!" Although my lower lids still twitched with imaginings of his pain, something about the victim's wan smile said he was wearing his red badge of courage to *look sympaty*. The female equivalent would have stayed home.

Children often saw men and women fighting. In fact, most of the time adults behave at least as idiotically as the *out o order pickney-dem* they constantly quarrelled with so what example had the children got?

The bus was packed as usual and tempers were not sweet. A man jumped in through the open door of the moving bus and swung himself into what seemed the last empty seat. He should have known better. He was suddenly accosted by an irate man.

"Lisn Iah, jus git up out o mi seat y'ear, Sah!"

"A wha yu a chat say bout a your seat?! A **public** bus dis, Star!"

"Me say git up, Man! Me **jus** git up go pay de man im money!"

"Dat a nuh fe mi business, Dread, **Me** fine dis seat **hempty!**"

"Me say it nuh **hempty**, man, **Me** was sittin' deh!"

"Well it nuh hempty now – HAH! HAH! HAH! - fe true!"

"Ey Man, yu wan me...?!"

"Wha yu a go do?! Wha yu a go do?!"

By this time the delighted bus load was raptly attending the rare spectacle of two men fighting over a bus seat.

"Me soon sidung pon yu!"

"Come den, nuh! Come den, nuh!"

The usurpee promptly sat in the usurper's lap. The bus load roared appreciatively.

"'Ey Man! Git up off o me! A wha do yu, Star?! A **desperate** yu desperate, nuh?! Heeyah, heeyah, heeyah!" the man laughed ..

"Me wan mi seat, Man... *Git up*!!!" The usurpee was really angry now.

"Mek me nuh, mek me nuh!"

"Me a go mek yu, yes!" He sat on the man, again.

I had wondered how the next bit had been so long in coming...

"*Is wha?! Is wha?!* Yu a BAttyman, nuh?!! HEEYAH, HEEYAH, HEEYAH!"

Having made sure the entire busload heard that one, there was the predictable, delighted uproar.

The usurpee continued his jack-in-the-box antics a while longer so as to impress the other passengers that he did not care for public opinion and then gave up.

You might have noticed that 'Sex' is a subject dear to the Jamaican heart, usually shrouded in heavily mixed feelings. Maybe this uncertainty is the reason that the subject is so loved in connection with high ridicule. One astute passenger acknowledged one of his equally on-the-ball brethren's knowledge of this fact.

"Yu see all like im? Im smart nuh rahtid yu know. Yu tink im woulda so rich if im never gwaan wid all dem slackness deh?"

"Yeah, an im a jive yellow BMW an all dem backside now. Me say Me ear some tings wha im a gwaan wid de odder day…an **Me…nuh…know**, y'ear Sah…!"

"Yu nuh know nuh! Well, **im know**! Jamaica people love slackness an im fine **dat rahtid out!** Yu stay deh!"

"But im doan ave nuh shame, eeh Sah? Mi God, an im a de ring doondoos too, yu know!"

"Mek me tell yu someting Dread, yu coulda did ave tree grow in a yu face – if yu gi Jamaica people-dem slackness, dem wi mek yu a rich man. Yu nuh ear when im go a foreign an aks de Jamaica people-dem wha dem wan ear, "…Culcha or Slackness?"…ow dem bawl out, "SLACKNESS! ! !"

"Me ear, Sah, Me ear!"

"Yu tink im fool, nuh? Im **sumart!**"

As a matter of fact, the DJ has so much influence that on one fantastically crowded bus, when a voice from the depths of the morass exclaimed, "Tek yu han out me pocket…!" someone's basic instinct said, "…Before me chop it!". The driver immediately confirmed my thoughts with, "Heh, Hayayayay! Im wan tun DJ now…'Tek yu han out o mi pocket!…'" he chanted on.

Sometimes it can really get dark though because even as one part of us is wrapped up in religion and things out of this world, so the other is very animal. One day something sounding like the usual colourful West Indian exaggeration turned out to be no joke.

"All like im shouldn live – im fe dead!" said a man. A woman answered, "**Dead??!! Dead??!!** Dem shoulda string im up, cut off im balls an pick out im toe nail-dem one by one!" They had been talking about the recent rape and murder of a child, uncommon then, more common now.

12

*Further Notes On
Behaviour & Broughtupsy*

As much as we've tried to set up a school bus system, our mixed attitude to youngsters causes everlasting problems with the transportation of school children.

We were thickly packed into a mini one morning. I was sandwiched in the middle so I could hear everything quite well. A man boarded. The conductor said to the nearest child, "Git up pickney! Stan up ere-so mek de man sidung."

An incensed woman at the back asked, "Ow yu mean fe tell de pickney say im mus get up?! Look ow long im deh-deh in a de corner not troublin a Gahd soul an yu a come talk bout im fe get up...**fe man?! Man, yu out o order!!**"

The new male passenger, now sitting as comfortably as the packed bus allowed, was unaware.

"When big people wan seat pickney fe git up."

"Ow yu mean?! Yu a come tell me say pickney an oman mus get up fe man?!"

"Chuh oman, shet yu mout an stap mek-up noise in people ais." Some people were looking at the sparring partners.

"**Naah!** Me **naah** shet mi mout, man, becau yu out o order. Yu nuh ear wha Missa Charles say?!"

"Mch! Listen oman, worse enough Missa Charles say pickney mus come in a de bus...but im **never** say dem fe get seat!"

"But Jeezas..." it was beyond her and, like a spark to kerosene, the rest of the passengers joined the fray.

There is another side to every coin. I once met a hard-pressed gentleman coming down out of Stony Hill in the afternoon in his clean-looking 'Hiace' van and I flagged him down.

"Half-way Tree?"

He nodded, "Come nuh," opening the front door for me. I got in with another woman he seemed to know. Something was funny though... A crisply dressed gentleman and a clean, well kept and empty vehicle, in mid-afternoon when it should have been rammed with school *pickney*.

"Yes Ma'am, de insurance money it a breed me...," he said to his acquaintance in the back. He looked pained, the eyebrows forming the upside-down 'V' that causes a person to look like he or she is permanently sighing.

"Me know ow de tings-dem high today me dear Sah."

"A tirty-six tousan dollar Me pay fe it two year ago, yu know, an Me barely a pay fe it now… Kyaan mek nuh money, man, kyaan mek nuh money. De gas, de insurance, de pickney-dem…" he looked beaten and resigned.

That last remark was a clue to what was bugging me about the whole thing.

To both of us now, "Oonu not in nuh urry? Me ave fe pick up some pickney before Me reach down a Alf-way Tree."

More pieces falling into place. We were passing Immaculate Conception High School.

"Yes Ma'am, de pickney-dem nowadays, dem out o order yu see. Me nuh know wha dem a go do wid de whole o dem, Sah. Dem doan ave no respec fe nuttin."

"Lahd Sah, a nuh me yu a tell!"

"Mi dear Ma'am, Me nuh come up a Immaculate one day fe pick up one likkle pickney an Me lock up de res o dem a mek up one someting inside de bus! Likkle mos some o dem pitch poopalick out de window! Me say! Dem **hout o horder!**"

"But wait…! Um-um…!" his friend intoned.

"Misiss! Me say when me come back… Dem nuh bruk out alf de window-dem an tear out de roof!"

"But see ere mi Gahd!"

Throughout his awful memories, the man's mouth remained dead-pan and the only hint that the situation might have exceeded even his limits was that the upside-down 'V' had completely disappeared into his receding hairline. Sometimes it really was a thankless world.

We had turned off Constant Spring Road onto Shortwood Road and seemed to be waiting forever for a *pickney* outside the gate of a little prep school. Finally, the driver's friend offered to go and get the child. Two children, a teacher and the driver's friend came back. Some kind of negotiation and explanation was going on. The extra little girl was apparently not scheduled for pick up. It was the usual story of a child left waiting till all hours and at the same time being expected to remain glued to the waiting spot so as not to keep people waiting whenever they did eventually collect him or her.

"Yu see all dat now," said the old gentleman, "Look ow long de teacher would ave fe sidung wid de pickney. Dem parents deh...**mchchch**...! An den when dem done now, yu know, dem bawl an scream ow de pickney-dem out o order an doan-care!" He gave the unscheduled child a ride.

We came to Half-way Tree and the man wouldn't accept any money from me. It all fell into place! He was the driver of one of the first *pickney* or school buses and on his way down, had seen a woman he knew. He had told me to hop in since I had also needed a drive. Why would he have become the driver of a pickney bus – and not for upper St. Andrew children alone, either? This was also long before the divestment of the JOS and the era of mini operators crying, "NO NO FRYERS! NO FRYERS!" – along with Transport Minister Charles' continual begging of them to take children. Who was paying this very kind and trustworthy older gentleman – and how much? Mysterious little miracles still happened.

SYSTEMS ANALYSIS

13

Collecting Passengers – or Not...

Passengers are mostly locked into the unfortunate trap of wanting to blow up the whole bus system while, at the same time, being totally dependent on it.

For example, in the evening rush hour somewhere out on the Spanish Town-Hagley Park Road route, a fair sized group of people was waiting on transport of any kind. One woman was waiting with a whole bankraful of mangoes which hadn't been sold that day. A *transpote* appeared on the horizon and she optimistically got ready for boarding, mango bankra in arms. The heavily laden bus shot past. She was stunned. Like lightning, a mango went zinging after the bus. Not far away two men were standing with their arms folded, talking casually. They noted the scene and one observed, "Eehi, see it deh now,...an if yu did beg er it she wouldn gi yu it, yu know..."

On another occasion, on the final 11.30 night run, a kind conductress of the former JOS saw what she made out to be a teenager flagging down the bus a little distance from the appointed stop. She signalled to make sure the driver slowed for him since it was the last bus.

The youth jumped in, said "Tank yu!" and held out his fare. The conductress stopped and frowned. He looked too old for the 20 cents and his style of dress didn't look school-uniformish enough. He didn't have a student ID card either. This card eventually died the expected death – they weren't really suited to Jamaican society.

"A mi school uniform dis!" said the boy.

The conductress wasn't sure. It may or may not have been a uniform – like the Jamaica College type, before people became used to its casual appearance.

By this time the driver was quarrelling about how, "...De whole o dem wicked an ungrateful an hole up de bus when people out o de goodness o dem art stop fe dem..." and he described some 'national fabric' for good measure.

The conductress finally allowed the boy in because it was late and lonely, but she kept telling him he was to, "...Wear im right uniform."

What with the casual looking uniforms, the many new private bus operators and the fact that boys and young men made khaki their uniform in or out of school; the problem became quite awful because most students were not disciplined into wearing the easily recognizable badge or tie.

"Plenty seat!" I often wondered if I were looking at the same scene that the crew of a packed bus was looking at. "Plenty seat!" usually means you may barely be able to wedge yourself in somewhere. I eventually discovered the real meaning of, "Whole heap o seat!"

I was climbing into a bus that I had resigned myself to take, packed or not. It was packed – people standing in the aisle, the conductor shouting, "Come dahlin, come, whole eap o seat!"

Side-winding my way in, I said, "Seat? Mus be for duppy!"

He pointed a hand, "See it deh!"

Backside, boy! There really were two empty seats! I quickly realised why though. One was over the engine casing and other was over the wheel cavity.

Sometimes – especially Sunday afternoons and mornings going to work – passengers would rather stand than move to claim less than comfortable seating, but oddly enough, only if the fault of discomfort lay with the original vehicle design and not with human crowding. They'd wedge themselves anywhere among people rather than sit with bent up legs or over a hot area in their good clothes.

I climbed over and sat in the engine seat and the smiling driver said to me, "Yu see seat, dough...?"

"Yeah, but das not plenty seat," I said.

"Den what? You can full up two seat, dough?"

"No."

"Den dat nuh whole eap o seat fe you?!"

Yes boy! I shut up. Faultless logic as usual. I had finally discovered the real standards for judging seating capacity. So much so that on the same bus on which the potential pick-pocket victim had delighted the DJ driver, I had had an idea of what was coming when the driver shouted, "Yeah man, im can squeeze in up ya-so!" But, this was special.

The driver opened the elevated door to his cubicle on the side of the bus opposite to the regular loading side. This meant he was loading from the middle to the teaming, afternoon, rush hour street – and not just one, but five people piled in! They stuck themselves anywhere they could around the driver, like cherries stuffed in a disorderly fashion around the base of a cake.

"Come Man, move yu foot mek de door shut!" said the driver. The men were flattened back against the inside of the rails and partition, which were supposed to ensure the driver safe operation space. A foot was planted on the dash board. An arm and hand wound out the window and around the' bracket of the wing mirror, while the driver skilfully preserved his unobstructed vision by directing the owner of the hand how to arrange himself. A body wedged itself between the edge of the driving cubicle partition and the bus wall, to which the partition was attached only by an overhead rail, Yet another body crooked itself forward over the driver's head.

Nothing is ever announced about the amount of room in an empty bus. It's probably illogical to think that the English Language could have a superlative or phrase vast enough in scope to describe that amount of room.

14

Their Fares...

The minibus comes tearing down at you – almost into you – madly flicking lights or bipping the horn. You are being notified that the bus will take you on as a passenger. If this is not meaningful enough, half of the conductor appears out of the window, sweeping the semaphore arm at the distal end of which is attached the ubiquitous fan of fares. He is shouting the destination at you and, "Plenty seat, man! Plenty seat in deh!"

When you observe, "I doan see any seat!" you may get, "Gway gyal! Press, driver! Alf-way Tree...! Alf-way Tree!" in reply. On a point of courtesy though, you were only addressed like that if you were the one stupid enough to flag down the packed mini in the first place.

The fan of bills is really a great system. There is a finger for each of the denominations so they can't get mixed up. Loop a wad around a finger and, 1 am informed, it is very difficult to steal. Within the curve of the palm of the same hand there was also usually protected, three columns of coins, again, each of a different denomination. A column might run from the heel of the hand as far as the ring knuckle, at which point the finger bends over the column, holding it like a clamp. It bore remarkable resemblance to a coin dispenser. The real virtuosas – the former JOS conductresses - may have held as many as four columns of coins in one palm and the columns may have extended to the final knuckle and, not only that, one column may have been divided into two or three denominations of coins!

The four-column business is now non-existent. It's-really a matter of inflation. In the heat of the fmancial chase, coin columns have given way to larger and larger bill fans.

Collection of fares in a packed bus is quite wonderful. Remember the mountain goat business earlier on? Well, another notable approach is the boa constrictor method employed by lots of minibus conductors. It's always the men.

Whenever the minibus stops at a convenient stop light or regular stop, the side door is pushed open and the conductor, feet still planted in the rear of the bus, snakes outside the bus, round the door stanchion and in through the front window; "Gi me some fare, nuh." When you're in the front and the face and dollar bill fan alone suddenly appear, inches from your own face – from the outside – it can be disconcerting. Then, just as sleekly, the vision withdraws and returns to its lair in the back.

If this method is too strenuous or if even years of practised writhing and impressive stretching cannot accommodate the size of the bus, the conductor hops out at the stoplight. He circles the bus like a playful dolphin frolicking around a ship and collects fares through the windows. He hops in just as the bus begins to move off.

Then there is the conveyor system most often used by conductresses. They stay put, except if the bus has stopped at a terminus when they may walk the aisle and collect. The money must come to them and the change is returned at the door when you leave, or, the transactions are done by a conveyor line of hands. In a very crowded bus, money comes to you, you know not whence nor where destined, but you pass it along. It will *reach*. Somewhere along the line, it could easily disappear into some strange pocket, but this never happened in my fourteen or so years on our buses.

The fares themselves are a very sore point. During my time, fares for adults went from something like 15 cents to $1.00 for three stages. To make the problem of the rising cost of living worse, the era of the minibus had been introduced by their ancestors, *de robut-dem*. Whenever the JOS was on strike these pirates extorted from the public whatever they liked. As the JOS was surely outstripped by demand for services and mismanaged into the ground on top of it, the robot became an established fact of life – something like the way black sea-eggs show up on a dying reef.

Since mini transport had arrived to stay, some kind of regulation had to be attempted. However, coming from lawless beginnings, habits remained ingrained and the road to management was and is rocky. The minis and their operators became synonymous with beating the system. It wasn't till the JOS completely gave up the ghost to divestment that any real control over fares, insurance, licensing, etc., occurred.

Apart from over-charging, all kinds of methods were used to extract more money from the public. A person had to do his very best to make sure that he had the correct fare. Please note that it had always been required of us by the JOS but only under duress do we Jamaicans put ourselves out to make things easier for everyone. Now, if the fare was 40 cents and you handed in a 50-cent coin, likely as not you would hear that that route cost 50 cents on that mini.

There were also innocent disembarkers who would pay $1.00 for an 80-cent fare. They were left with hands outstretched and mouths gaping as the bus jerked away.

"Nuh ave nuh change, man, nuh ave nuh change! Nex time! Nex time!"

The conductor would slyly have done a little coin shuffling, apparently searching for change. The constantly revving engine would have given the conductor an excuse to hop the bus again, hopefully implying that the driver might have left him if he'd hung around. However, everyone knows that this idea is ridiculous because a conductor never gets left. A highly developed sixth sense precludes such an occurrence. There are times when a conductor is absent from his vehicle and nowhere in sight until after the first gear has been drawn. He mysteriously reappears hanging from the doorway.

It followed that the nearer your actual payment was to the established fare, the greater the danger of there being, "No change!" since your payment was just a little over the set fare. However, all

Jamaicans know the risk involved in blatantly taking advantage of a largish sum of a person's money. I saw more women than men succumb to this one.

To prevent these things from happening, it was important to know your facts. If you could say you had read in the Gleaner what fares should be, or, that you had checked with the Ministry, the fare transaction often went in your favour. I found it worked very well. Nevertheless, when the latter didn't work, there were other self-protection tactics, but you had to exercise good strategic judgement. If you paid your fare early you had the entire bus ride to haggle with the conductor and apply enough pressure to cause him to resort to honesty, for a peaceful life. The conductor also could not just dash away with the change or have such.an easy hand in over-charging you if he was surrounded by the public eye. You should also have done everything possible to pay your fare while still inside the bus and not on the sidewalk.

Few conductors collected from you as you entered the bus. The general collection zone was just before the first major stop on a given route. Matilda's Corner fills this bill on the run from Half-way Tree to Papine and back. Everybody who got off before the collection zone was expected to hand over their fares just before or upon leaving the bus. However, since life is a two- way street, some passengers outsmarted operators - but very rarely.

One day, around the Kingsway intersection on Hope Road, a man got off the bus in the regular way then made a terrific break for it and dashed away down the sidewalk. The conductor tore after him and no one completely realised what was happening until we heard the driver cursing, "De fuckin kine o tief wha dem ave a run up an down nowadays...Lef im an come, Man! Mek im gwaan!"

The conductor gave up the chase when the delinquent jumped a wall and disappeared into some scrubby open land. The very annoyed conductor, whose ego was miffed, returned breathing hard and cursing in a meaningful way. He collected all fares.

Personality has a lot to do with a person's success – passenger's or conductor's. The more you could convince a person that you were in control, the better your chances of winning. Monkey often knew which tree to climb. The judgement came not only in deciding what personality type you were dealing with but also in a decision on the road worthiness of your transportation. It was inadvisable to pay a fare early in a very dilapidated vehicle as you might not get where you were going and private entrepreneurs rarely returned fares.

Another trick used to extract money from the unsuspecting was more subtle and probably fool proof. Two different groups of passengers were involved, many of whom were not personally ripped off. Yet, all contributed to the lining of the *tiefing* operators' pockets. A relatively small number became direct victims of rip-off in this scheme. Now follow the strategy carefully.

A certain group of drivers would illegally divide a non-stop route into two. Their original legal agreement might have stated that their route was a direct one, for example, the non-stop route from downtown to rural Golden Spring. However, they would divide it in two at Constant Spring, the last corporate area stop before the foothills of St. Andrew where Golden Spring lies. To get away with the above *lampsing*, mini operators had to make sure the stage was set with a couple of prerequisites. First, there had to be an obvious, logical reason for dividing one route into two – in this case both topographical and civic boundaries - and second, the point of division had to be a big, bustling stop or terminus where maximum confusion was an excellent smoke-screen. It also helped that there were two other groups of operators which had legally agreed to divide the route into two – one taking the corporate, the other, the the rural leg. Furthemore, in the early days, the public had no way of knowing which of the three groups was which. The whole scheme of the illegal operators naturally meant that they were also cutting in on fellow minibus crews' earnings.

For local routes, the Downtown-Golden Spring run legally had six stages. If it was run as a non-stop route, the fare was cheaper if you paid all six stages at one time rather than stage by stage. Knowing this fact full well, the samfie crew would end their designated non-stop route at the third stage – Constant Spring – regardless. All passengers were off-loaded. Then, a new set of lambs was picked up for the Constant Spring- Golden Spring run. The passenger who was directly ripped off was the one going the full route but who was deliberately misled. Downtown, the *samfie* non-stop route men had tricked him into believing that their bus route terminated at Constant Spring. To get to Golden Spring he now had to pay for a further three stages at local route prices, thereby inflating the cost of the whole trip.

I am happy to say that this practice died out. Regulation grew longer teeth. It seems most of the overcharging and rip-off problems with fares have now been cleared up with the advent of a private system of transport associations and companies. However, fare-stage designations and routing were for a long time screwed up by various crews hoping to make that little bit extra.

15

...& Their Baggage

Besides the special methodology and psychology of collecting fares and passengers, baggage collection also needs a special approach and skill. On country buses, conductors are usually balancing artists of a supreme order and nowhere can you see it better than during the loading of bankra, bunches, bundles, bulging sacks, bursting grips, bits of furniture and tyres.

Someone outside the bus might yell that he needs to load *someting*. The *someting* might be an ever-spreading sea of produce stretching as far as the eye can see and completely encircling the passenger. All in a day's work, the country-bus conductor bounds out of the bus door, scales the side of the bus and, Tarzan-like, lopes onto the roof. If the bus is too crowded for it to be worth fighting towards the door, or, if the window just seems a handier exit, the responding conductor dives forwards out the window and, cat-like, twists round, face up, so he sits on the windowsill. He then grasps the rim of the roof or the cargo rack brackets and pulls himself up from the window until his feet rest on the sill. Then he either springs backwards onto the pavement or launches himself onto the roof. It's so stupid...so daring...so graceful.

In the harmony of technique special to loaders the world over, the massive cargo is swung up to the roof, caught and packed with a heavy grace. An assisting passenger and the conductor look vigorous and their breathing heaves in time with the strenuous motion. The movement is oiled and precise so they look like mechanised mannequins.

As the load piles higher and stretches farther across the roof, the mountain goat comes out in the conductor or sometimes the involved passenger. The passenger may do roof duty instead of the conductor who then handles sidewalk operations. Whoever is on the roof must ensure firmly balanced footing amidst, beside and over the mounting cargo so that he is not hauled to the ground by the weights he is catching. Next, he must hop over and around the cargo, lashing it down, while being careful not to mash produce with a carelessly placed foot. If things are really hectic, even a conscientious driver might pitch in, but rarely.

If the person with the massive baggage is a woman, it is usually the conductor and some helpful male bystander or fellow passenger who helps her with her load.

The nearer the bus to Kingston, the less welcome the large load because the passengers become more and more urbane and less and less concerned with marketing produce – unless of course it's a known market day or an accepted market transportation vehicle. The loading and unloading holds up the vehicle and passengers begin complaining loudly. They have to bear long stops before their destinations. The situation is particularly tense when a person, late for market, meets up with the clerical nine-to-fivers heading for their offices. The employees get *antsy* about being late, although of course they are not actually worried about punctuality at work. If the produce is piled into, instead of on top of the bus in order not to waste time, the danger of staining *cris* clothes and scuffing clean shoes becomes very real. There is then unpleasantness. The marketer keeps up a string of apologies and pacifying statements or she puts on truculent armour and ignores her way into the crowded bus amidst grumbling and complaining. On the urban runs, then, two car tyres or two stuffed bankras or boxes are about the limit; more than that and *yu deh pon yu own* as to whether the bus is going to pass you by because you're clearly being unreasonable.

On the really rural buses, of course, the bag and baggage is an accepted part of life and bus crews go to considerable lengths to make things as convenient as possible for everyone. For example, they might detour all over creation to stop as near your destination as possible. Sometimes city folk fly past their nests though. Imagine a driver detouring to Sangster International and then being asked by a porter to leave his bus to help unload baggage. Needless to say, not a soul paid the porter any mind.

16

Communication...in The Nation

"ONE STAP JIVER!"

In Jamaica, apart from the DJ's knack with rhyme and rhythm, communication is generally high art and science. For example, if you were standing with your back to two children who were talking and one said to the other, "...An im kibber im an so!" How would you figure the meaning? That the person had covered his hand in a certain way? Even if you've got past *kibber*, which means *cover* – you're **wrong**! I know so because I saw it. Most of the time you have to see and hear Jamaicans talk to catch the meaning.

As the girl spoke, she showed the other one how some person had flung up an arm and ducked his head under it to protect himself from something that had suddenly come at him.

Keeping in mind that *an* = *hand* = *arm*, the real meaning of her statement was, "...And he put up his arm to cover his head like this!" Oh, one more thing...don't assume the girl was talking about a male, either – *im* can mean *er*.

Drivers, conductors and passengers have a specialised communication system.

In a Leyland bus there is a bell that must be 'pressed once' to notify the driver that a passenger wants to get off. However, for us unequivocal Jamaicans, a bell must be rung at least twice. The conductress or conductor also used to have a buzzer which only he or she could use to notify the driver to open the doors, close them, start off, etc. Nevertheless, the conductors and passengers had back-up systems in case the original ones failed and also used these back-ups to add emphasis.

A passenger whose 'ting-ting' is not always heard – due to the roaring engines or packed conditions or out of order bell – or all three – can always just bawl, "STAP DE BUS!!!" The conductress was usually the first to pick up the cry of distress and, rather than use the unimpressive buzzer or bell, she resorted to the far more urgent sound of the ten-cent piece clacking against the bus railing. It wasn't the stupid little new ones that she used either. How far a driver had shot past the stop was reflected in the tone and volume of the passenger's voice – not to mention his language – and in the frequency and loudness of the coin staccato.

There were certain situations in which the buzzer never came into play. For example, if a passenger had run the 100-yd. dash and braved being knocked flat by on-coming traffic rather than miss the bus that was just moving off, or, if a school bag or some piece of clothing was slammed in the hydraulic doors, the coin came into immediate use.

With all the hanging around bus doors it's a wonder there aren't ten times more entrapment accidents – the odd one is, sadly, fatal.

The buzzer was sometimes used to signal for door opening, but only after the bus had long since stopped. Even so, the buzzer was more usually associated with door closure and move-off.

Minis and privately owned non-Leyland buses may have had buzzers for stopping the vehicles, but other signal forms were far more common.

"One stop, Jiver!" or "Bus-stop, Jiver!" are communications for disembarking. Other communications regarding disembarkation and boarding are:

"Hole down, Jiver!"

"Tek one, Jiver!"

"Tek up!"

"YOW! YOW!"

"Let off!"

"Stan up, mi Boss! Stan up!"

"Hole on, Jiver!"

"Sekkle! Sekkle!"

"Leggo one!"

Conductors had an equally elaborate and possibly more cryptic range of communications for telling drivers they might proceed. These included:

"Lif up!"

"Fly!"

"Dash!"

"Flash it"

"BUS!"

"Go way!"

"Draw way!"

"Raise up!"

"Bubble!"

"Lick shot, Jiver!"

"Press!"

"Go tru, Jiver!"

On country buses and beat-up or, at least, well used mini-buses; a loud, tinny bashing of the bus side is often substituted for verbal commands to stop and go. At times, it is astoundingly thunderous and dented areas can be found just beside the doorways – especially on the buses on which the conductor uses his foot instead of the flat of his hand.

On all privately owned buses, particularly the minis, the rate of fly past at the various stops was far higher than with the JOS – hence more shouting, bad language, swerving and drawing of brakes.

17

Road Code

Driving habits of public transportation drivers are *dread* all over the developing world and in some free spirited European countries as well. Here, we set standards of *dreadness*, especially since every category of Jamaican road user can be *dread*. The laws governing road use and public transportation are supposed to protect everybody, but our public vehicles' crews don't really see it that way. They feel these rules are an infringement of personal rights; an attempt to *keep down de small man* and generally a damn' nuisance. Never mind him having made as much as $200,000 a year, for a long time, tax free. 'Body Protruding' used to be a special nuisance.

It's a real credit to authorities that the minis are finally beginning to acknowledge use of earlier JOS bus stops instead of just pulling over anywhere to let off and take on passengers. However, the way buses pull into or move off from a stop, totally oblivious of traffic around them, will never be cured. Bus drivers know that drivers of cars and all smaller vehicles will stop and *mek dem go tru*. However, the mood is noticeably more cautious around fellow *transpotes*.

An unwitting motorist coming up to a bus stop might suddenly notice the screaming of a high-revving engine going into compression behind him, an ear-splitting, predatory "BEEEEEEEEEEEEP!!!" and a presence looming close by. Most unnerving. The minibus, once it's established its supremacy in the pecking order, overtakes and recklessly swerves in front of the desperately stopped private vehicle whose driver now leans mercilessly on his horn and uses language. As a token acknowledgement of the road code, the bus's indicator is sometimes flashed maybe twice when it is pulling across the motorist's path – two seconds before a dead stop. Otherwise, the conductor's arm might shoot out of the door with the usual fan of dollar bills sticking out between the fingers as an indicator.

The moving off process is very similar and, from a traffic helicopter, must look like a mad movie. The mini pulls away from the curb without warning, the car behind it pulls farther out to avoid hitting the mini and the reckless driver of the vehicle behind that first desperate car – not wanting to bother with unnecessary hold-ups – pulls still farther out into on-coming traffic. On-coming vehicles screech to a halt or swerve violently to the left to avoid what, at every minute, seems a sure thing and yet, somehow, never happens. Every driver curses every other driver for good measure...and life goes on.

Another credit to the authorities is the fact that fewer *ductors* ride the sides and doors of their vehicles as compared to those who squash themselves into a seat or stand inside and continue to risk a rare and harmless case of 'Body Protruding' – only a bottom out of a window. After all, our regulatory entities do know just how far they can push rules.

Occasional spot checks on vehicles became part of the new transportation regulation system. It was a good idea but, done the Jamaican way, it was as inconvenient and dangerous as possible – in the middle of afternoon rush hour traffic. People milled about everywhere and crowded into buses, dying to go home. Forget testing depots.

Just as my packed bus was moving out of the Constant Spring terminus, a man jumped in and ordered everyone out saying, "Me a go tes it!". Grumbling and cursing, everyone got out. The man took the empty bus and roared around to the wide pavement behind the market. Don't you know what was coming... The bus, once a luxury tourist liner, shot into view and then pitched to a laboured halt. Sure enough, the stock racers of Baja California were a foolishness to this man. It seemed a bit much even to the ousted driver – "Watch wha im a do wid it now, nuh." The tester jack started the big bus, screwed it round in impossibly tight circles, changed through all gears in a 200-yard space and skidded to rubber-burning stops. It did seem the brakes were a little slow in taking effect, though.

After the required demonstration of authority and skill, the tester bore down on the curb causing a wave of backward movement and cursing among the alarmed, waiting passengers. Smoke and fumes swirled round the entire chassis as the tester jumped out and confronted the uneasy driver.

"De brake-dem doan good," was the decisive verdict. Some arrangement, other than bribery, may have been made because no money changed hands that day and the shirty driver was allowed to reload his bus and go.

18

When It Bruk Down...

When it *bruk down*, fix it – and not a minute before.

When it comes to road code and mechanical operation of public motor vehicles in Jamaica, no other underlying belief system would make sense. External symptoms usually match internal states of affairs very closely and transportation is no exception. Engines often have to be left running and accelerators gunned constantly to prevent shut down. Headlights blow fuses regularly and engines belch out great black gobs of diesel smoke...and still they run...up hill and down dale, even over the horrendous roads of rural St. Andrew. The relative number of breakdowns is strangely minimal and are most common after a stop.

Road conditions are murderous, but drivers acknowledge this point of view only if they are driving privately owned vehicles. There are pits to navigate, near boulders to surmount and ripples and trenches to hurdle. The ripples were dug up by passing bulldozers going to construction sites in the country. There are also the flash deluges that pour over the roads and rush away over the hillsides and into gullies and then, last but not least, there are the telephone company and water authorities... Oh well, can't have it all, eh.

The Jollies, even when fully loaded – as only the developing world knows how to load – were extraordinarily manoeuvrable for their size and weight. They passed over incredibly precipitous and tortuous roads. The uninitiated – like new Peace Corps workers – find it hair-raising.

Leyland and whoever makes the country buses should be proud of their buses. Jamaica is these companies' testing ground, no need for experimental facilities. We tax our buses to the limit. It's obvious minis and vans don't have the staying power of the big buses because mini numbers have dwindled noticeably, but that doesn't stop us squeezing out their last juice of life. Some fall apart on the way to wherever or shudder to a halt never to start again or just plain blow up.

Once we were *bubbling* down Hope Road and came to an abrupt stop at the Abbey Court intersection. The mini's unlocked door shot backwards and just kept on going, right off its runners, and crashed onto the road. The conductor exclaimed mildly and laughed. The driver only twisted to see what had happened. Unphased, the conductor jumped out, picked up the door, re- inserted it between the runners and got back into the bus, a restraining hand on the prodigal door. All this before the light turned green.

Another time, on the way down Constant Spring Road, in a mini of unknown make – looked like an old bread van – I had only been subconsciously noticing the exceptional extraction work the driver was performing on the teeth of his gears. I guess immunity must set in some time. As the situation got worse I began really paying attention. At every stoplight the hauling and grinding intensified. Finally, the van simply would not budge.

"Hm. Mus e wan fluid," the conductor remarked. A man who can ply a route from beyond Stony Hill to town without attending to clutch fluid is a mark of the breed.

On yet another trip between Half-way Tree and Papine, we were coming down to Lane Supermarket in a traffic jam. People in the front of my mini saw it first.

"Rass...! Look deh...! De someting blow up!" I craned my neck and, sure enough, fearsome black clouds were billowing up, blocking all view. "Den a whe de fire-chuck deh?! De tyre-dem a go burs!" I got frightened; I hadn't thought of that. With a shock I could now see the sad little van dying in a furious nest of brilliant orange flame. Were people in it?! There was no median then so our driver tried to turn across the road and go through Lane Plaza to avoid driving by the burning van. Unfortunately, whichever way we went took us roughly the same distance to it. The traffic jam was the deciding factor and our driver turned the wheel back to go straight ahead. I was petrified. The driver went very wide, but still not wide enough if a tyre exploded hurling flame in all directions. It was awesome passing that much flame so close, especially with a strong wind whipping it to a frenzy. If the blaze changed direction it could easily have reached us. My heart was in my mouth. Mine was a window seat closest to the burning van. It was mesmerizing.

Mercifully we passed without problems, but the picture of the little van stayed with me. They drove those little vehicles into the ground – just like their donkeys – and then cursed them or wondered why when they didn't perform. News shouted to us through the windows while we had been in the jam told us that no one even got a scratch. Some luck, boy!

As mentioned before, drivers become notorious for how they drive their vehicles – but only if the handling is truly appalling or dangerous. They also have some less obvious idiosyncrasies, again, to do with changing gears and other modus operandi. However, one driver was very well known for his gear technique so it necessarily followed that this technique was horrific. He and some others simply didn't know how to drive and had no sense of how a gear box worked. They hove away from a stop sending passengers reeling backwards; raised their feet off the accelerator as if it were 40-ton spring loaded, pitching passengers forwards; then found another gear and flung the people back again. They hauled in second gear just after the bus had shuddered to a stop while struggling up an incline.

The effect was really marked in a semi-crowded or empty bus or one with nowhere you could hang on. In the empty buses, people spent the trip staggering about like drunks. In the semi-crowded buses, passengers were subject to the domino effect and feet and baggage on the floor were regularly mashed. If a hand didn't find something to grab onto in time to save its owner from being pitched about, the *leggo* hand might often almost haul off someone's clothing or clap somebody a good one.

The kind of driver being dealt with here also had no regard for people who might be trying to seat and arrange themselves for move off. In the days of the JOS, the conductress usually knew her skipper and often told passengers to "Hole on! Hole on!" or "Sidung! Sidung!". This kind of driver brought seats to meet rear ends with a massive jarring of the spine. Crying out, people were deposited like flour sacks. Naturally, these truly deficient drivers were subject to much cursing and many insults, but they had acquired immunity syndrome – 'AIS' – ironically.

"Ey, Bwoy! A nuh cow y'a jive yu know!"

"A whe yu buy yu licen, Bwoy?! Yu shouldn jive fowl, much less...!"

These drivers stayed in business because there was often no choice if you wanted to reach your home.

It must really be damn' boring driving up and down all day long though, so making driving a unique personal expression and developing your own style could be a way of preventing humdrum.

A Leyland bus had a good solid gear lever casing while country buses have unsheathed levers that looked like reedy stalks blowing in the wind. These willow-in-the-wind gear sticks are long and often bent up around and forwards over an engine casing. Once engaged, this kind of stick might sway on a radius of as much as ten to twenty inches without disengaging itself. How the drivers manage is uncertain, but they seem to develop a sense of which way the stick will sway depending on curve and camber of the road. However, I've seen hands come down only to discover no stick where it was thought to be. A quick fishing around and the located stick is shifted without looking or pausing.

Drivers sometimes change gears with a hooked index finger. A hooked index finger looking for a wayward gear stick belongs on 'Candid Camera'. The crook of the wrist rested on the gear stick ball is another manipulation technique. There are also true virtuosos. They crash in gears and swoop down on the knobs like maestros completing a keyboard concerto. This style requires the use of an open hand, the gear knob fitting just into the curve formed by the relaxed ring, middle and index fingers. Some drivers handle the gear knob as if it were truly disgusting. No more than fingertips contact the knob.

The public also makes a concerted contribution to wear and tear. One way that society frequently expressed itself upon the JOS was by knifing or ripping up the bus seats. In the oldest buses – all gone now – the stuffing, partly made of coir, would pop out and *stick-up* the passengers if they didn't notice the tear before sitting. When a seat was torn, passengers only used it under extreme hardship. As time passed the JOS overcame this problem with the new moulded fibre-glass seat.

Gone are the days of knifing and ripping; only a small amount of cracking, chipping, carving, scratching and breaking continues. You really have to badly want to express yourself to affect fibre-glass – it's just not worth the effort.

This kind of vandalism could feasibly be committed by people kept waiting for up to two hours at an unsheltered bus-stop at midday, after two previous bus changes – but it never is. It's the idlers who do it.

The old upholstered seats and back rests were often dislodged by hard use and this still sometimes happens with the fibre-glass ones. Furthermore, it's not once or twice I saw the entire iron framework of the seats broken out of the former JOS buses.

We used to crack up laughing on the verandah at home because I told my family there was a way to tell if the Jollies had people in their back bench seats or not. When they stopped on Monterey Drive outside our house, whether they were being recklessly driven or not, "BOOF!" meant there were no passengers in the back seat to keep the dislodged back rest in place. We heard the thudding on the bus floor regularly.

19

Terminal Anarchy

Every major bus terminus in Jamaica has its history. Each has its own name and many were once resting places for horse and buggy travellers going back and forth across the island. Examples are Parade, Cross Roads, Half-way Tree and Constant Spring. All the names have obvious roots. Parade was the old army parade ground, Cross Roads needs no explanation, a constant spring is behind the Constant Spring Golf Course and at Half-way Tree there was once a giant and favourite shade tree which roughly marked the half-way point between town and country. 'Country' then is now upper St. Andrew.

At these places, markets sprang up for a ready-made clientele. Then came the rum-bar and hardware store, and as the town square grew into a traffic centre, all the other necessary consumer outlets were added. Many squares grew into complete towns. When the omnibus first came to Jamaica in the form of the 'chi-chi 'White' bus' – hydraulic doors went "Chchch!" and 'White' was the manufacturer – it followed its ancestor, the tramcar, and fitted into the historical scheme. The square kept adding new vehicular elements to its traffic flow and was called a terminus by the various transport associations.

Many other elements of society can also claim a bus terminus as their terminus – stray animals, passengers *lookin a lif*, vendors, hangers-on, taxis, mad people and *pickney* all make the terminus a rendezvous point on their various routes. These elements mix and mingle haphazardly and it's a miracle half of them aren't knocked down or killed in the melee. When the buses careen into a terminus it's every man for himself. True, Jamaicans are noted jay-walkers, but it's not unusual to see sidewalk users leaping backwards to avoid drivers racing to within a terrifying inch of the curb. It's quite nerve wracking and strong oaths always follow.

Despite valiant attempts at regulation and monitoring, a terminus looks like a disturbed wasp's nest. At major ones, the old squares have been rearranged and divided in order to allow traffic to flow freely in one direction only and let the buses of certain routes use given areas of the square as their exclusive stops. Good theory. Unfortunately, the authorities just haven't been able to deal with the umpteen grey areas presented them by country buses, taxis, push-carts and minibuses that won't stick to designated areas. Minis, big buses and other vehicles often park two and three abreast, or even four, completely blocking the road.

The sustained racket at the terminus is punctuated by the horns of minis trying to make headway through the morass or by horns of others ready for loading. Therefore, horns are useless due to cry-wolf syndrome and are ignored in times of real need. Nearly as loud as the horns are the decibel levels of route and destination announcements and of the peculiar running courtship of potential passengers. However, natural market forces and clearer route designations have reduced the need for criers.

"PAPINE...pap out! SEE IT YA, READY BUS DIS! PAPINE BUS ERE! PAPINE, PAP OUT! PAPINE, PAP OUT!" He had decided he liked his little ditty, but the passengers did *pap out* if move-off of their chosen mini was excessively delayed by the song and dance of the conductor.

"SPRING!" another common cry. "SPRING BUS DIS!" This bus was headed for Constant Spring.

Speaking of Constant Spring, there was an afternoon at that place when I and about four other people beside me nearly jumped out of our skins with fright.

"M O U N T A I R Y ! ! ! !" a voice boomed. It was incredible! When something causes a whole group of Jamaicans in a crowded area to stop, look, raise eyebrows and even laugh in shocked surprise, it's either a fight or something beyond extraordinary. The natural volume and tone of the man's voice was astounding. One woman actually corked her ears as she passed. The man was only a hanger-on, but he had quickly recognised his true calling – excuse the pun – and was obligingly putting himself at the disposal of the minibus operators.

"M O U N T A I R Y ! ! ! !" Indescribable. Nasal? Guttural? Both? Booming, without question. Mighty Thor had never so rocked Valhalla.

When there is just one van going in their direction, passengers abide anything to catch it. They rarely had their pick, but when they did, the scene was completely different, especially when the prospective passengers were female. Minis mostly had all-male crews and the conductors scurried up and down the sidewalk announcing their van. In hopes of demonstrating how ready their mini was to leave – even if it was obviously empty and with all the world knowing that empty minis go nowhere – the conductors jumped in and out of the vans like jack-in-the-boxes to show they were on the verge of moving off. The driver did his part by revving up the engine and driving two feet or just giving a jerk forwards before settling back at the curb.

Conductors sometimes left their vans and walked clear into the square to solicit business. They opened doors and fell all over themselves with courtesy towards women. The women were confronted by as many as three males all vying for her business. They shouted, used soft endearments, pranced about, bowed low and as the natural order requires, the female kept them all guessing. Her eyes remained unwavering, her course unswerving, and then, at the last minute, she veered and got into the mini of her choice. The other conductors whom she thwarted occasionally cursed her but usually just turned their sights on new quarry.

These aren't the only sources of auditory stimulation at a terminus, though. At most of the big ones there are two or three music outlets going full blast. Sometimes you can also stop for a heated effort at upliftment of your soul. The *pryer meetn* brings drums, chants, spiritual harangues and tambourines. The hosts are in white if it's a group. If it's a single burning evangelist, all he or she needs is the Bible, usually not even that since it's completely memorized anyway. The individual evangelist can appear day or night. The group is strictly an evening thing.

At Constant Spring there was once even a steel band worthy of any J'ouvert. It was nice to see that by then we were worldly enough for the band to really get our attention. Running through the whole orchestration was the all-pervasive pedestrian chorus, "Escuse! Escuse!" as commuters bored their way through the mob. The peanut man's *fiefie* normally edged the background sub-tumult.

On Fridays there may be Crown & Anchor men and other types whom moral society has decided are unsavoury. Other kinds of *unsavouries* are present all week long and they do become nuisances at times, like the loiterer being discussed while I was sitting in a mini at Half-way Tree. We were waiting out the usual rigmarole of pretense which precedes actual move off. The driver, who was a big, *crusty-back* type, but neatly dressed, was sitting at his wheel, one arm across the back of the seat, thumb of the other hand inserted well up his nostril. He observed, "Yu see all dem wha nuh ave nuh wuk? Dem jus sidung an fuck wid yu all day long."

His conductor replied, "An Me know im too, yu know. Me done tell im say aready nuh fe romp wid me!"

These gentlemen seemed very level and coolly able to handle everything but sometimes limits are over-stepped. On a late evening at Constant Spring, when everyone thought it was really time for the JOS to *carry people go a dem yard*, a young man was sitting beside a young lady on the bus. She had a window seat. They seemed to know each other well and the young fellow even seemed a little protective. He was dressed in the customary cut-off pants, *sojier* boot, Derby, etc. Tempers had become slightly short due to the wait, but the young man's own seemed soothed by the presence of the young lady.

Outside, it was guinep season and a *yout* in school uniform was indulging himself while making a thorough mess of the place. He threw skins and spat seeds till he began making a game of it. How far, how high, how accurate, etc. He was aiming at the bus side because it made a noise and, when skilfully done, caused a powerful ricochet. Unfortunately, he missed this time and uttered, "Wha...?!" as the wet pink seed fell, "Plip!" into the young lady's lap, inside the bus. She jumped, made a face of revulsion and batted the thing away. In a flash, her chivalrous companion leapt across her and pointing the notorious Jamaican index finger of menace out the window, bawled, "**Ey, Bwoy! Yu wan me come out deh come cut yu??!!**" Mercifully, the bus began to move off and the offending *yout* dashed away hollering semi-lunatic laughter.

Another unsavoury type who is less common at the terminus is the *ore* or loose woman. Due to continuing double standards, she is the worst kind of all and, not so ironically, it's the men who pick on her most loudly.

"Ey, Gyal! Yu nuh ave nuh yard fe go?!

The man was leaning against a minibus with one hand, his legs crossed at the ankles. The other hand was comfortably at rest, not in that common place of repose, the pocket; but in that other common Jamaican and Mexican place, the crotch. At the top of his voice he was addressing a shadowy figure in white seated at the Constant Spring rum-bar across the road.

"Gway! Me say go a yu yard!"

A willowy young lady standing not far from me hid an embarrassed laugh.

"What yu ave deh man nuh want again – I T U S E O U T!!!"

The young lady beside me said, "Lahd Gahd, a nuh me yu know; she nuh ave no shame. Watch ow she in deh a drink like man, nuh. She better dan me."

"Mondeh, Chewsdeh, Wensdeh, Tursdeh, Frideh LAHD, OMAN! GO A YU YARD GO RES IT...! I T S T R E T C H O U T! ! ! ! ALL YU DO A WALK STREET AN FUCK MAN! Walk an fuck! Walk an fuck!...GO OME!"

My first reaction had been shocked laughter when I realised what was going on, but as the well dressed woman left the bar and slipped quietly into the shadows behind the building, I felt depressed...and the white clothing was ironic.

Retail is a thriving business at a terminus. You can get almost anything with very little effort. The merchandise is regularly brought to the windows of the waiting bus and into it as well. Available commodities include household provisions, sky juice, barbequed chicken, toiletries, shoes, luxury items like costume jewelry, panties, etc. "KEESKO! KEESKO!" used to be a familiar cry. A novel sales pitch I once heard for 'Bubble Boy' bubble gum went like this – "Bubble gum, bubble gum! Bubble boy, bubble girl! Bubble up yu gum bubble boy, bubble girl!"

Another man who people thought was *alf crack*, sold fruit on the buses. His head was *picky-picky* and he wore long shorts – or short pants. In a weirdly rasping, nasal tone adopted for sales purposes he walked up and down the aisle announcing, "ARINGE! ARINGE!" His hard-sell also included the story of a real or fictitious woman *oo lef im*, and, he made some connection between the woman's leaving him and the reason you should buy his oranges. If she were real he could have gone mad because she had left him, but then again, his problem might have been the cause and not the result.

He wasn't a wholesome looking character and the very common, very sharp knife owned by all orange vendors seemed a little menacing in his hands, especially in the close quarters of the bus. Some women laughed nervously at him and men cussed him to, "Cumoff de bus an stap bodder-bodder-up de people-dem!" It really got uneasy when he chose a poor young girl to harass with his ware and "Dear John" saga. He eventually left us in peace with the bus load making much comment about how, "Im mus e mad an wan lock up."

As he went, I realised that all that ever really made a terminus crowd stop were the fights.

The bus rolled out towards home. The place would be a hive until about eleven o'clock and then go silent, only to wake up the next morning at about six o'clock. The country terminuses would by alive by four…

APPENDIX A

Names of Mini & Medium-size Buses

Double Dutch Bus
UFO
Disco 3000
Green
Wheels
Trying Man
Birth Control
Exterminator
Exterminator II
Turbo Charge
Super Star
John D
Love Bird
Lady Bird
Ready Tours
Upseter Tours
Double Dutch Bus
Hark of the Hills* (accompanied by paintings of two hawks)

Names of Big Buses

Five Points (A star is implied by accompanying drawing)
Israel
Victor
Two Sister
Uncle Sonny's Transport
Long Island
Moore's Transport
Three Brothers
North Liner
Flowers of Blessing

Mayfair
Buzz
Suzette
Riding West
National Queen
Rose of Sharon
Mail Bus
Sweet Heart Tours
Honey Bee
Morning Glory
Hard Worker
Uncle Sammy
** All names spelled as seen*

APPENDIX B*

Instructions

Do not speak to the driver

No rasta OR dread in dis bus!! (Seen in a north coast bus - a crew member explained that these types never pay their fares)

Used tickets here

Seating capacity 41

Standing capacity 44

Two is better than too many

Press once (bell)

Passengers leave moving vehicle at their own risk

Have correct fare ready

Demand a ticket from the conductor

Tag your baggage

No smoking

No spitting

No food or drink

Do not slam door

No profane language

NO RASS IN DIS BUS

Thoughts For The Day

You can take my money
You can take my wife
But if you take my van
Man,
You're fucking with your life
Trouble Dad a cup a tea
Do it with a vanner
We're hornier
Repent – The Lord is at hand
The Lord is my Shepherd,
Home
Shall I Fear...
Happiness is a warm pussy
If you're Rusty or Smutty...
You're a Sick Sugar Cane
Replant! Replant! Replant!
Welcome to 'Riding West' (in a bas-relief welding job in the metal floor plate near the door)

All statements were painted, inscribed or sculpted into or onto the bus's interiors or exteriors.

GLOSSARY

A

a – I, is, be, am, are; it is, there are (can imply ~ing of continuous present); to; of; in; at; have

air – air; hair

ais – ear(s)

aks – ask

alf – half (~-way Tree)

an – and; hand

antsy – irritated, like swarming ants

anyow – anyhow

appen – happen

ard – hard

aready -already

art – heart

av – have

awright – alright

B

baby-modder – common law mother

bade-off – bathe

bag-an-pan – see *caroaches*

bankra – square-corneredbasket made of palm thatch,
now loosely used for all large thatched hampers and baskets

bare – only

batty-man – homosexual (in Jamaica, batty – nates and
anus)

bax – box

becau – because

bes – best

bickle – food, victuals

bodder-bodder-up – bother, molest continously

booga – crepe sole, sneaker, tennis shoe; nasal mucus

bout – about

butu – ill-bred, unwholesome & unwelcome person

bubble – bubble; speed, accelerate

buil – build

burs – burst, explode, break

bwoy – boy

C

caroaches – encumbrances; bits and pieces; sundry items
usually viewed as valueless except to owner

chouble – trouble

chuch – church

chuh – expletive used like *tch*

chupidness – stupidness

claht – word used as a noun in profane Jamaican speech (probably a reference to loin underwear/female monthly sanitation material)

cumoff – come off

comin – coming

coo – look

Coolie – East Indian or person with this ehtnic appearance, only (in Jamaica)

crack – mad (cracked)

cris – pretty, handsome, good-looking

crown and anchor man – roadside croupier, often dishonest

culcha – culture, the civilised norm

cut-eye – malevolent side long glance, may also be teasing

D

dahlin – darling

darkers – sun-glasses

dat – that; pork

de – the

deestent – decent

deh – there (~-deh – has been there)

dem – them (~self – themselves); they; their (also fe-~ – their/s); these, those; ~-dem – the plural *s*

den – then

dis – this

doan – don't (~care – careless)

doin – doing

doondoos – albino

dough – though; dough

dread – man who may or may not be of Rastafarian faith, has long matted hair; dreadful, horrendous, usually both, used in and stemming from, biblical sense of something that inspires awe, as in "*The Lord is dreadful to thine eyes*"

dung – down

duppy – ghost

E

e – be
eap – heap
ear – hear; year
ccdiot – idiot
eehi – yes
Encaba – Encava trademark of Venezuelan buses
er – her

ere, ere-so – here
escuse – excuse (me)
ey – hey

F

facety – rude, impudent, arrogant
fas – fast, quick, quickly; interfering, meddlesome, quick to be nosy; rude
fe – for; to; (~-dem – their/s)
fifi – shrill steam whistle of the peanut vendor's cart, whistle, fife
fine – fine; find
fire-chuck – fire-truck
foo-foo – foolish (fool-fool)
foot – foot; feet; thigh; leg
frien – friend
fryer – child

G

Gahd -God
gi – give
govment – government
gwaan – go on, continue
gway – go away
gwine – going
gyal – girl

H

ha – have
han – hand; arm; and
hempty – empty

hole – hole; hold; old
horder – order
hout – out
hu-rass – extra emphasis on *rass* (see *rass*)

I

Iah – Man; my friend, etc., form of address thought to stem from Rastafarian philosophy of collective conciousness in which another person is seen as part of a single life force and is therefore also addressed as 'I'

illside – hillside

Im – him, her; his; he, she

J

J'ouvert – Monday before Ash Wednesday and start of Trinidad's Carnival, (probably from the French, *jour ouvert* – opening day)

JOS – Jamaica Omnibus Service (Jolly ~ – PR department's name and cartoon entity for the company)

jus – just

K

Keesko – Kisko, trade name for popular frozen novelty
ketch – catch(es), caught
kine – kind
kiss teeth – suck posterior surface of teeth to show disgust, real/playful
kyaan – cannot

L

labbrish – chat, share information, gossip
Labourite – member of Jamaica Labour Party
Lahd – Lord
lamps – con, cheat
leggo – let go; wild
licen – licence
lif – lift
likkle – little
llow – allow
los – lost

M

Ma – Ma'am, Madame

Mas – Master, Mister (often friendly)

Massa – Master, Sir; my friend

mch – usually a sound of disgust or annoyance, real or playful, known as kissing the teeth, which is roughly how the sound is made, can be prolonged

Me – I (~'d – I would [Me would])

meetn – meeting

mek – make, making; allow

member – remember; member

mi – my

mine – mine; mind

Misiss – Madame (Mistress)

Missa – Mister

moully – mouldy; of unpleasant aspect

mout – mouth (~-water – saliva; gun-~ – rifle barrel, narrow)

mus – must

N

naah – not; am/is/are not, will not; no (rarer, emphatic).

naygah – Negro, used to describe individual of any race disparagingly, but can be friendly/teasing among social equals

neider – neither

nex – next

no – no; any

nowhe – nowhere

nuh – any; didn't (but); (am/is/are) not; do not/does not; (am I/is it/are they) not (like/so)?; (why) don't (you)?

nuistance – nuisance

nuttin – nothing

O

o – of

odder – other

og – hog

otahiti apple – ruby coloured, pear shaped, lightly sweet fruit with a rose essence (possibly from the French *au Tahiti* – of Tahiti

ole – old; hole; hold

oman – woman

ome – home

oo – who

ook-worm – hook-worm, intestinal parasite

oonu – you (plural)

ot – hot

ow – how

P

pack-up – packed

payin – paying

pickney – child(ren)

picky-picky – untidy, uncombed, in small tufts, usually referring to very short negroid hair which may now be a deliberate style produced to follow street fashion or to emulate style of native African origin

PNP – People's National Party

pon – at, on, upon

poopalick – sommersault

poppy show – a public spectacle, an embarassment, ridiculous (possibly from puppet show, after the old European street entertainment custom which often ridiculed real people)

pryer – prayer

puss-eye – light-coloured eyes, sometimes slanted

R

rahtid – (vulg not profane) used as noun, adjective, verb, adverb and expletive

ram-up – rammed, packed to the limit

rass – (profane) used as noun, adjective, verb, adverb and expletive, may be used offensively or fondly, in awe or disgust (frequently ~ clabt), probably originally a contraction of 'your ass'

res – rest

ring – ring; absolute, real, true

robut – robot; name given to small vehicles used for illegal public transportation

rudie – delinquent, criminal

rung – round, around (~about – roundabout, traffic circle)

S

sah – sir

samfie – con, cheat

sekkle – settle, be still, stop

sellin – selling

shet – shut

shub – shove

sidung – sit down

sittin – sitting

sky juice – syrup over shaved ice

slackness – vulgarity, profanity

smaddy – person, someone, somebody

small-up – make small (~ yuself – make yourself/yourselves small)

smilin – smiling (~ wid -flirting)

sof – soft

sojier – soldier

St. Elizabeth Red – person from parish of St. Elizabeth of German or mixed Afro- German heritage, reference to their sun burned skin colour

stan – stand

stap – stop

sumart – smart

T

tan – tan; stand
tank – tank; thank
tegereg – rough, uncouth, trouble-maker
tek – take
tief – thief (~ing – thieving)
till – till; still
ting – thing
tink – think; stink
trash – dried leaves used as packing material, waste
trow – throw
tru – true; through
tump – thump
tun – turn
tung – town

U

ungle – only

ungry – hungry
urry – hurry

W

wan – want
way – way; away
we – we; us
wha – what
whe – where
wi – will
wid – with
wiss – vine used for basket weaving
worl – world
wuk – work

Y

ya, ya-so – here
yaah – you hear
yard – yard; home
yout – youth
yu, y' – you

About the Author

Integrative General Practitioner, Transformational Coach & Counsellor. Danced 34 years including semi-professional work. You can also find me at http://pinterest.com/onlinejamPublisher of:YU GET JOOK! Diaries of a Jamaican Medic.SHUB DOWN & SMALL-UP YUSELF! Diaries of Jamaica by Bus

Read more at www.OnlineCounsellingJamaica.com.

About the Publisher

Polar Bear Press - A unique partnership bred the animal. Publisher of:YU GET JOOK! Diaries of a Jamaican Medic.SHUB DOWN & SMALL-UP YUSELF! Diaries of Jamaica by Bus

www.ingramcontent.com/pod-product-compliance
Lightning Source LLC
Chambersburg PA
CBHW020526160726
47992CB00005BA/2266